# LITTLE THINGS, BIG THINGS

## THE PURSUIT OF CALM AND CONTENTMENT IN THE EVERYDAY MOMENTS

SWARNALI NATH

*Dedicated to everyone learning the mantra to live, laugh, and love*

# Contents


*Epigraph* — vii

*Acknowledgements* — ix

*Preface* — xi

1. Listening To The Morning Birdsong With Gökotta — 1

2. Walking At Your Own Pace With Oubaitori — 5

3. Questioning The Inner Child And Receiving Answers With Sisu — 9

4. Defining The Purpose Of Life With Ikigai — 13

5. Letting Go And Moving On With Pyt — 17

6. Practicing The Art Of Acceptance With Ukeireru — 21

7. Finding The Beauty In Imperfection With Wabi-Sabi — 25

8. Finding Strength In Brokenness With Kintsugi — 28

9. Practicing Gratitude With Kansha — 32

10. Practicing Compassion With Omoiyari — 36

11. Perceiving The World Around With Nunchi — 39

12. Contemplating The Pause With Ikebana — 42

13. Finding A Glimpse Of Yourself With Meraki — 45

14. Getting Into Self-improvement With Kaizen — 48

15. Finding Happiness At The Job With Arbejdsglæde — 53

16. Taking A Break From Work With Fika — 56

17. Giving Value To Your Leisure Time With Susegad — 59

18. Turning The Online Mode Off With Koselig — 62

19. Connecting To Nature With Friluftsliv — 65

20. Traveling To The Forest With Shinrin-yoku — 68

21. Calming Down Your Anxious Mind With Mångata — 72

22. Living A Balanced Life With Lagom — 75

# Contents


23. Resting Your Mind-Body-Soul With Niksen     79

24. Surrendering Yourself To The Natural Flow With Wu Wei     85

25. Cherishing The Joy Of Little Things With Hygge     90

26. Celebrating Everyday Happiness With Lykke     93

27. Giving Importance To Every Moment With Ichigo Ichie     96

28. Realizing The Zeal Of Life With Kefi     100

A Livsnjutare Sings!     105

Bibliography     107

References     111

Author's Note     131

About the Author     133

Also by the Author     135

Praise for the Book     137

# Epigraph

*Far from the hustle and bustle of life, you may hear a sound – the music of silence, the whispering breeze, or the rustle of fallen leaves; they may want to tell you what is forgotten and forsaken – celebrating the little things.*

# Acknowledgements

I convey my sincere gratitude and regards to the Holy Trio: Thakur Sri Ramakrishna Paramhansadev, Holy Mother Sri Sarada Devi, and Swami Vivekananda. Their blessings motivate me to keep going, defy all the challenges, and learn new aspects of life every day.

I thank my parents and sister for their unwavering support in my writing endeavors. Thanks to them, I can dedicate myself to the pursuit of happiness through my literary offerings.

I am eternally grateful to my women's tribe, circle of writers, and community of bloggers—everyone who reads my work and leaves valuable feedback, sometimes correcting my mistakes, sometimes improving my writing, and other times encouraging me to follow my heart and explore new avenues in creativity. For these wonderful people, I continue working in the field of Mindful Living, where I have successfully carved my niche by gifting my readers moments of calm and contentment.

Last but not the least, I thank the universe for protecting my peace and allowing me to learn these wonderful concepts of living life to the fullest.

# Preface

**The Song of Psithurism**
Maybe this life is all about
Listening to the birdsong in the morning,
Perhaps, it is all about
seeking a glimpse of life's hidden meanings.
Perhaps, it is all about
finding the colors of spring.
Or, maybe, it is all about
savoring a meal,
hugging the trees,
touching the sunbeams,
and within the process, learning to heal.
Perhaps, this life is all about,
finding the way to laugh, love, and live.

I research ways of finding peace in our everyday moments. I like to work on the theme of finding calm in chaos. Surprisingly, the more I research, the more I realize that we often ignore the reminder that holds a mirror to the truth. There is peace in little things, there is peace in slow living, and we can find happiness in ordinary things that may seem nothing to hold any importance. These mundane things can help you come alive from the long passage of despair, and bring you happiness in the most unpredictable way, and this is why I started this book with the song of Psithurism. The word 'Psithurism' means the rustling sound of leaves. One can hear the music of the falling leaves only when they embrace slow living and find calm and contentment in little things, and this is the message I tried to convey through my book.

Within the everyday moments, there is a glimpse of your blissful self—your still, calm, tranquil self that has always been with you, even to the point of your utmost ignorance. All you need is to stop, stare, and discover the blissful truths hidden in yourself.

In this book, I have discussed 28 concepts and philosophies that teach us how to discover peace and happiness in everyday life as they reveal the secrets of well-being worldwide.

Thus, 'Little Things, Big Things' reminds my readers that the pursuit of calm and contentment in everyday moments begins with the ordinary things that are often left unseen. These things come to us at the right hour when we search for inner peace and happiness. I hope my book reminds you of the forgotten and forsaken 'little things', and their connection to the 'big things' by sharing the wisdom to embrace a happy and peaceful life.

# CHAPTER ONE

# Listening to the Morning Birdsong with Gökotta

The morning whispers to me
That it has something to offer me
a smile
a song
or perhaps, the wind of tranquility.
But I forget everything
When I listen to the blissful music
That the bird songs bring to me.
Dancing on the trees,
they sing me the song of peace.

Since my childhood, I have been privileged to live in places where I had opportunities to hear birdsongs. Many birds visited us to bring the message of a new dawn. Now, I wake up every morning listening to the sweet chirping of the birds that visit our garden in the early dawn hours. Tailor Birds, House Sparrows, Doves, Bulbuls, Parrots, Mynas, Magpie Robin, Asian Koels, Pigeons – although I spend my day with their sweet cacophony, the birdsongs in early dawn seem the most peaceful song that whispers a prayer of gratitude and a promise of hope.

Before I leave my bed and prepare to start the day, I watch sunrays peeking through the curtains, telling me that it's time for another new beginning. With this peaceful invitation, I listen to the sweet symphony of birds. They fill my heart with calm and contentment, and I welcome the new day with a note of gratitude and appreciation.

I wake up to the bird songs, go to the garden, and embrace the stillness of the early morning hour. The silence in nature, the healing vibes of the morning, and witnessing the earth preparing for a new beginning, everything seems blissful.

~

When your day starts with this sweet chirping of birds and calmness around, your heart will be filled with a serene bliss. This is what we can practice with the art of listening to the bird song in the early morning - Gökotta (pronounced *zyohh- kot – tah*), a Swedish word that means rising in the early morning hour to listen to the bird song.

If you go outside and engage in watching the birds sing their first songs in the early hours of dawn, when the Sun is rising and the first sun rays are touching the earth, this wonderful sight fills your heart with joy, relieving your stress and rejuvenating you to begin the new day!

In some regions of Sweden, there is a beautiful tradition where the people go out into the woods on Ascension Day which comes 40 days after Easter. They do this because they want to listen to the birds in the woods. Especially, they wish to hear the cuckoo sing – they want to cherish the moments of listening to the cuckoo's first song in Spring.

In Sweden, Gökotta encapsulates the act of rising early to relish these serene moments, to commune with nature and oneself before the hustle and bustle of daily life takes over. But Gökotta is more than simply waking up early — it's a profound philosophy that encourages mindfulness, gratitude, and an appreciation for the quiet beauty and wonder surrounding us. It's about carving out a pocket of tranquility in a fast-paced world, where we can pause, breathe, and absorb the magic of existence.

At its core, Gökotta is a reminder to embrace the present moment. In a world often dominated by deadlines and distractions, this Swedish philosophy invites us to slow down and savor the simple joys that usually go unnoticed in our hurried routines.

To practice the art of listening to birdsongs in the dawn hours, you need to prepare your mind to be an early riser so you never miss the bird songs in the early morning hour. Waking up, go to the garden or park or any place where there are ample trees and birds, and then, surrender yourself to the blissful serenity of the morning. Grow the habit of mindful listening to listen to the sweet chirpings. Feel the breeze and allow yourself to embrace the stillness within this tranquility. Never rush in your Gökotta hour; instead, savor the moments to feel the peace around you. Don't stress your mind with thoughts, rather, try to declutter all the burdening thoughts that occupied your mind for a long.

When you incorporate this art into your daily life, it will help to calm down your morning anxiety. Moreover, your morning will start with a blissful note that helps to keep your mind away from all the worries and anxious thoughts.

Another beautiful aspect of practicing this art is it is a wonderful way to immerse yourself in nature that further helps uplift your mental and emotional well-being. Listening to bird songs and watching the sight of birds dancing and singing in the early morning hours promote positivity and increase productivity. The sweet chirpings of birds offer a sense of calm that significantly helps reduce stress. Moreover, if observed mindfully, the birdsongs have a specific rhythm and melodic pattern which creates soothing and relaxing vibes in mind.

The uplifting melody of birdsongs makes a positive impact on your overall well-being. Practicing the art of listening to birdsongs in the early morning will help you feel calm and content because of the inner joy and peace. The beautiful harmonies of birdsongs and the calming atmosphere in nature create a profound sense of serenity and tranquility. It also helps in enhancing your cognitive functioning by providing improved focus and attention. The rhythmic patterns of the melody produced in the birdsongs significantly help create a restorative effect on your mental resources, thus offering you a chance for rejuvenation by improving your cognitive abilities and combatting mental fatigue.

Most importantly, waking up early in the dawn hours and going to nature to listen to the birdsongs offer moments to nurture a sense of awe through bird watching, discovering, and reconnecting with yourself with a profound sense of contentment.

When you develop the habit of practicing Gökotta, your mornings will start with more peace and calmness. After practicing this beautiful art, you will see that your mornings have become more purposeful.

After all, morning shows the day, and with the beautiful art of Gökotta, your morning will show you the purpose of life!

# CHAPTER TWO

# Walking at Your Own Pace with Oubaitori

Every season has its own blooms
To offer the earth their smiles
of peace and happiness.

There is peace in living with yourself—no rush, no hustle, only to celebrate your progress and growth in your own way. Slowly, silently, secretly, like you have been watering the plant of self-growth every day with hope and faith that someday, it will bloom, and then, one day, it blooms.

It feels peaceful - watching the flower bloom at its own pace, unfurling its petals with all its uniqueness.

You are happy, proud, and surprised. You are happy to see that the wait is finally rewarded with the blossoms of resilience. You are proud to see that the blossoms gracefully dwindle in the breeze, whispering your journey to the strangers. You are surprised to see its beauty – the patterns, the colors, the layers, everything reflecting the beauty of faith and the grace in surrendering.

This is how a tree teaches us to grow at our own pace and celebrate every step of the progress. When you give yourself time to bloom, it becomes a blissful journey of surrendering yourself to the universe and trusting its plan. You may wait for the season of blossoms and each day, eagerness may fill your heart, but deep down, you are calm, still, and hopeful of the truth that when the right time comes, you will bloom with your uniqueness.

I learned this lesson from Oubaitori (pronounced *oh-buy-toe-ree*) – an ancient Japanese idiom that teaches us how staying hopeful about the outcome and walking at your own pace can give you peace of mind and the joy of celebrating your growth.

Oubaitori, a Japanese Idiom comes from the kanji for the four trees that bloom in spring. The trees are: cherry blossoms, plum, peach, and apricot. Each flower on this earth has its own season and time to bloom. Thus, the idiom tells us it is peaceful to know that everyone has their own timing: that we all grow and bloom at our own pace.

Though these four trees co-exist alongside each other, each of them has something unique – the colors of the flowers are different, they have a specific order, and most beautifully, they have their own time to bloom. Thus, the season of Spring looks like a riot of colors, yet, these trees look like the queen of their own empire, allowing themselves to prepare and gift the season with their blooms.

When I came across this beautiful idiom, my restlessness calmed down within moments. Oubaitori acted like a gentle reminder for me, that it is okay if I am working and walking at my own pace. If I stop comparing myself with my peers, then my mind will be calmer than before. No matter how much effort I may put into something, it will happen only in its own time - if you can accept this fact, then walking through life's path becomes easier.

Most importantly, when you stop comparing yourself with others following the Oubaitori way, unbeknownst to you, there opens a door to the universe because you surrender yourself to your inner guide. Within the slow pace and stillness, you learn to celebrate your growth and see the blessings you are gifted with – your uniqueness – the treasures that were left unseen.

To practice Oubaitori in your everyday life, you must focus on your uniqueness and embrace your individuality. Avoid comparing your life path with others. Instead, celebrate your own journey and personal growth. Focus on mastering the craft rather than comparing your life with others' timelines.

Accepting the truth that everyone has their own timing according to the universe's plans is the first step towards integrating happiness and peace into your life when you are walking on the Oubaitori path.

Mindful self-reflection, conscious living, and present-moment awareness are three key aspects of Oubaitori. You must set personal goals that align with your higher purpose in life and find harmony with your values and ethics.

Cultivate self-compassion and gratitude for having the uniqueness that defines you. Engage in positive self-talk and use positive affirmations to encourage your growth. Honor your self-worth. Most importantly, constantly remind yourself of the truth that all along the journey, you are working, and you are walking at your own pace towards your goal. All your efforts are being counted, and thus, they will bloom in their own season, reflecting your uniqueness by rewarding you with the most beautiful blossom.

Oubaitori reminds you of the essential truths to find calm and contentment in life. It acts as a reminder to nurture your own unique talent, have faith in yourself, trust the universe's plan, and embrace the stillness within. Water the hope in your heart every day, praise every little step, affirm yourself with messages of optimism and self-love, and be grateful for all the blessings you receive. Address your strengths, channelize your potential, and believe that in the end, everything falls into place.

This way, walking at your own pace in the Oubaitori way, you celebrate yourself every day, and witness the changing colors of Spring within.

Isn't it the most beautiful teaching from nature?

# CHAPTER THREE

# Questioning the Inner Child and Receiving Answers with Sisu

I gather the fragments of my soul,
to become whole again.
They echo my story of resilience
and remind me of my strength.

During my research for this book, I was awestruck by the incredible concepts about life. Sisu was undoubtedly one of them.

I remember I was dwelling in a conflict and confused about my decision. It was night and I was preparing for sleep. But somehow, I was reluctant to go to sleep and instead, I kept searching for the wellness concepts to write on my book.

Meanwhile, I came across the Finnish word Sisu, and it instantly grabbed my attention. When I learned about the Sisu mindset, gradually, I fell in love with this brilliant art of resilience and perseverance.

If you ask your inner self to take the plunge into the thing where lies your passion, what would you tell the self? 'Just do it.' This is what Sisu tells us. For Finns, the word Sisu is something more than just a word. It is embodied as a part of their character and lifestyle.

The word Sisu (pronounced *see-soo*) first appeared in an issue of Time magazine in 1940. In simple English, the word Sisu means grit, inner strength, and courage. It is a wonderful way to believe in your inner strength and trust your heart's call.

Sisu is a mystical force that spells the magic of resilience and perseverance. It's the superpower you carefully preserve for the toughest times, fighting challenges with your utmost determination. When you reach the threshold of your capacity and desperately seek the strength to bounce back, Sisu offers you that inner strength to endure every pain you go through and help you overcome adversities.

Sisu is the victory song that sings your story of survival and success.

Eventually, your determination and perseverance will bring you calm even if you are dwelling amidst the conflicts of making your decision. With the help of the Sisu mindset, we can defy the odds to face difficulties with the utmost resilience. With the power of perseverance, we can do any job with extreme endurance and strong determination.

Since I learned about Sisu, it has helped me a lot to choose the right path and stick to my decisions. Sisu helped me to follow the path that I wanted to follow, putting my heart and soul into it. It also helped me to be firm with the decisions that I made.

Being a Bengali, the word Sisu instantly made a personal connection because, in Bengali, Sisu means child. This is why I wanted to interpret the Sisu mindset on my own and started incorporating Sisu into my daily life as a tool to connect with my inner child and gather strength, courage, and endurance from the purest truths echoed to me from within.

For me, practicing Sisu is all about trusting my intuition in the form of the answers from my inner child.

Here is how I do this:

I slow down and give myself time to process the overwhelming feelings.

Then, sitting in quietude, I take a deep breath and question my inner child. I wait for the answers to remind and affirm myself of my true potential. After some moments, I try to hear the voice of my inner child. In the whisper from my heart, I hear a voice telling me what I forgot about myself – a message of compassion, endurance, and determination.

Sometimes, my inner child sends me signals. I manifest the signals I receive from the purest and truest part of me because it always feels the right thing to do in my adversities.

When I started practicing Sisu, gradually I learned how to turn inward and seek the guidance of my inner child. Instead of panicking, now I try to calm down my mind and work towards my purpose with the utmost resilience. In adverse situations, I tell myself that it is time to embrace the Sisu mindset to overcome this challenging time.

Many times, it helped me recognize my inner strength, boost my enthusiasm, and motivate me to cling to hope. 'Hold on a little longer' - this is what my inner child sings whenever I am in difficulties.

I am grateful for the moment when I discovered Sisu. Now, whenever I am in a conflict, I close my eyes and ask my inner child the question that causes the turbulence in me. I hear the voice answering me with the guidance to show me the path that embodies my purpose in life, and it offers me a sense of order within the chaos, and harmony with the universe.

Isn't it beautiful to celebrate the everlasting childhood in your heart in the form of Sisu? Don't we all want the inner child to live in us forever?

# CHAPTER FOUR

# Defining the Purpose of Life with Ikigai

I find my peace in working with a purpose
That keeps me going
to work with a meaning
As it reminds me
of the reason for my being.

Often you forget to work on your purpose in life, but when things fall apart, only the sense of purposefulness can give you peace of mind - to remind you of this truth, I have brought the wonderful concept that teaches us the importance of finding the meaning of our being.

Ikigai (pronounced *ee-kee-gahy*) is a beautiful Japanese concept that reminds everyone on this earth has a purpose behind their existence.

Ikigai is a combination of two terms; *iki* which means alive or life, and *gai* which means benefit or worth. Therefore, combining these two terms gives us Ikigai, which means finding your life's purpose or meaning. In short, Ikigai means finding your purpose for being alive. The French term *raison d'etre* shares a similar meaning to Ikigai, as these two mean the same thing —reason for being.

Pursuing your Ikigai offers you a greater sense of calm and contentment because deep down, you know that you are working according to the universe's guidance. Fulfilling your purpose naturally calms your restlessness and aligns your material purpose with your spiritual purpose. Thus, you become an instrument of the divine power that guides you ahead to serve the world with your best capabilities.

When you pursue your purpose in life, you wake up to joy every morning—this indicates that you have certainly found your Ikigai. Once you find your Ikigai, nothing can stop you from achieving success because you work towards your higher purpose, and every day, you take one more step toward self-improvement.

For me, the concept of Ikigai is as vast as the universe and as deep as the soul.

Ikigai is a state of mind and well-being where you learn about the true purpose in life. The Ikigai state can arise from a devotion to your favorite activities that you like to do with all your passion. You enjoy doing the job, never get bored, and that job offers you moments of calm and contentment. Thus, you find a true sense of fulfillment in your being, and as a result, your Ikigai becomes the reason why you get up from your bed in the morning.

Ikigai miraculously helps with self-reflection, identifying core values, exploring new opportunities, setting goals for future endeavors, decluttering unnecessary baggage, and improving focus on matters of the utmost importance. Pursuing your Ikigai also helps with mindfulness because you do things more mindfully with undivided attention.

When you become more aware of your reason for being, you realize and recognize the process of becoming.

Find your Ikigai - this may sound very easy, but when you go on your hunt for finding the purpose in life, or more precisely, finding your Ikigai, this may seem more difficult than said. Because we live in such a lifestyle where we only focus on our bigger goals. Doing a lot of work, being more productive, learning different skills, being a master of everything we do, earning more and being more successful than we desire, being happy with our relationships, and the list never ends.

As a result, we forget to enjoy the little things. We also forget to ask ourselves, "What brings me peace?" We are oblivious to the fact that such questions make us pause and ponder upon the way of living, and most importantly, they question our being which in turn helps in addressing the root and contribute to the process of becoming.

Therefore, if you want to find your Ikigai, pause and ask yourself the questions that answer your reason for being.

One day, take a break from your life's daily tasks, or you can also do it on your holiday. Sit in a lonely corner of your home and ask yourself,

1. What brings you happiness?
2. What brings you contentment?
3. What brings you fulfillment?
4. What is the thing that pushes you out of your bed every morning, and makes you do it without thinking twice?
5. What is the job that makes you feel your aliveness to the extreme?

While finding the answers to the above questions, there may come only one word as your answer. Because, for me, it was writing and whenever I ask these questions to my inner self, I only find the answer, "writing".

Among these questions, the last question makes me think of the deepest of my soul. Because I have been there on the other side of life when I lost any hope for tomorrow, but thankfully, writing was there to bring me back to the light and make me come alive. And I still remember the moment when it happened. It was like someone whispered to my ears, touched my soul, and gifted me a boon of rebirth.

Isn't it true for everyone who has found their Ikigai?

# CHAPTER FIVE

# Letting Go and Moving on with Pyt

I forget
I forgive
I let go
and ask my pain
to water the seed
of purpose and peace.

Suppose you feel frustrated amidst your hectic life routine, and something happens that makes you angry. You are unable to control the situation. What will you do at that time?

Well, I will Pyt.

Pyt (pronounced *pid)* is essentially a cultural concept that is hugely practiced in Denmark. Essentially, it is a way of cultivating healthy thoughts that will help you deal with your stressful life. However, Pyt is more of a habit that makes us learn the act of letting go. Whenever we want to forget the past, we often tell ourselves to let it go. Whether it is a grieving memory, a moment of heartbreak, slipping from the ladder of success, or broken relationships and a nightmare that carried a lot more like these, we often say to ourselves, 'Let it go.'

This is the Pyt way of saying 'Let it go'. The Danish people would like to say 'Pyt med det' which means 'Don't worry about it' or simply 'It doesn't matter'. Try to say 'Pyt met det', it feels peaceful saying to yourself 'Just forget it, and better you let it go.'

If you are too attached to something that is making you angry, stressed, or frustrated, the situation can go out of control as you might do something that you should not do. And what will happen next? Your mind will lose all its calm.

But, just think for once, if you can ignore it and move on instead of staying there, you walk ahead to your own purpose in life. You let it go, and allow yourself to welcome peace to your life.

Here lies the secret of Pyt.

When you delve deeper, Pyt is the art of letting go mindfully and moving on purposefully. This is how you can find a sense of peace and purpose when you incorporate the Pyt principles into your life.

Here is how I practice the art of letting go by integrating the concept of Pyt.

In the first module of practicing Pyt, it requires three steps: self-exploration, self-analysis, and self-reflection. In the next module, Pyt needs to be practiced through non-attachment, present-moment awareness, and finally, letting go.

First Module:

In the first step, I give time to myself for self-exploration. I introspect myself and my current situation, try to figure out the stressors and address the pointers that help me recognize the root cause of the turmoil.

Then, I sit for self-analysis. After a thorough analysis of my thoughts, emotions, moods, behaviors, and needs, I write the findings in my journal. After the steps of self-exploration and self-analysis, I go for self-assessment and note down the outcomes of this introspection.

Finally, I reflect on the takeaways and try to understand my subconscious mind more deeply.

After the first module, I take a pause and allow myself to rest, and then, I try to engage in some mindful activities like mindful walking, doodling, mindful breathing etc. to release the angst and pain that I was carrying within.

Second Module:

Once the first module is over and I am back to the practice after a brief pause, now, it's my time to practice non-attachment. In this step, I detach myself from the outcomes and allow myself to welcome the experiences and changes without judgment. This time, I focus on my spiritual quests and look inward to introspect my inner self that is dwelling within, somewhere detached from the material world.

**Surprisingly, this practice gives me peace and calms down my restlessness by transforming my inner chaos into a harmonious melody.**

Slowly, I bring my senses and focus to the present moment and practice gratitude, self-compassion, and acceptance. After practicing this step, my heart fills with peace, and I see the flower of purpose blooming in me.

Gradually, I grow an optimistic outlook on everything, nurture a greater sense of awareness, embrace tranquility, and develop a fresh perspective to start anew.

Finally, I let go of the past and step ahead to move on.

Thus, I integrate the concept of Pyt as a tool for mindfulness practice which helps in my mental, emotional, and spiritual well-being.

~

Often, we stay in the same thing for a long period, and as a result, the situation becomes worse over time. The same has happened in my life. I have learned from those lessons that sometimes, the best way to find peace is to ignore the chaotic situation, and slowly move on. This is what Pyt reminds me of, whenever I forget to focus on the higher goals in life. I learned that if we can ignore the situation that is becoming worse if we stay longer, there is a possibility of losing control of anger. At that moment, it is better to just ignore it, and leave it as it is. Thus, I skipped the stressful situation and calmed down my anxious mind by practicing the art of letting go following the Pyt way. It also helped me in resetting my brain with a positive mindset.

Sometimes, it seems too difficult for me to forget my past and stop regretting the bygone days. However, as I have learned the art of letting go by practicing the beautiful concept of Pyt, now I prefer to embrace it to pursue my higher purpose. Whenever I feel sad thinking about my past, I tell myself, 'Who cares? Just say, 'Pyt', because it is time to move on.'

Are you sailing on the same boat?

Let's say 'Pyt med det' together!

# CHAPTER SIX

# Practicing the Art of Acceptance with Ukeireru

The door of acceptance opens in me
the door of survival,
transformation,
and rebirth.

When it comes to acceptance, you need to be at peace; when peace comes, slowly, there comes harmony - the harmony that helps you to understand the eternal connection between every being on earth.

When I started my Life Coaching studies, the first course that I did was Mindfulness studies. When I started learning and practicing mindfulness in my daily life, the first step of my Mindfulness journey was Accepting.

If you start living mindfully, then you will gradually become aware of the magic of living with present-moment awareness. From my experience, I discovered that accepting is the key to inner peace. If we can practice the art of acceptance, we will find peace amidst the chaos, and this is what Ukeireru teaches us.

Ukeireru (pronounced *oo-kay-reh-roo*) is a Japanese concept of acceptance. It is a culture that helps us learn how to give value to acceptance. It is a way of life that introduces us to the art of acceptance. Whether it is small or big, you will see the difference when you start embracing the art of acceptance.

I have started accepting everything to the extent it is possible for me. Since I am on my way to acceptance, I have stopped regretting the things that did not serve my purpose. I have experienced that now I am more into acceptance, and it helps me calm down my mind.

To practice Ukeireru, you need to mindfully observe your surroundings and develop a non-judgmental mindset. With a positive outlook, you must accept every situation in your life. In addition, you can practice gratitude, connect with yourself through nature walks, and follow conscious living. To practice the art of acceptance, deep breathing exercises are also helpful.

Pause, breathe, and reflect on everything. Allow yourself to accept everything that has been bothering you so far, and then remind yourself that you have let go of the past so that you can be completely present in this moment. Using positive affirmations that act like a reminder of the truth—acceptance is peace—profoundly helps you live with inner calm.

Ukeireru is significantly connected to well-being. Following the Ukeireru way of practicing acceptance offers you a sense of being mindfully aware of your presence – in the world, in society, in nature, in your home, and your own being. First, you have to accept reality, no matter how tough your reality is, you have to accept it so that you can let go of the burdening facts and thoughts. Not only introspection but also a profound observation of the world around you - how it is connected to you, how it shares a bond with you, how it impacts you, and how these all factors hold importance for you.

During my practice of the art of acceptance, at some moments of self-realization, I discover that when I see the world around me and ponder upon the fact that how important they are for me or vice-versa, I feel peace because these moments of self-realization make me aware of the importance of the self. Sometimes, I become angry or upset about the situation or I feel sad receiving some harsh words from someone in my circle, but the next moment, I feel lighter when I emphasize the fact that they don't serve any purpose to me nor do they hold any importance for me, and in such situations, you realize how beautifully we co-exist in a world where at the end, all we need is to prioritize self-awareness. As a result, you will have more room for calm and contentment because now you know yourself better.

Beyond self-acceptance, this art encourages me to ponder upon the vastness of life and living with harmony.

Accepting is hard, sometimes, it feels very difficult, but it is not an impossible thing. Accepting does not mean you are allowing the world to do whatever they wish, or you need to accept everything irrespective of your choice. However, if you can accept yourself more and accept the universe being your inner guide – gradually, you see, everything falls in place. This is how the art of acceptance offers you peace. Slowly, you may find new avenues to explore, and trusting the universe's signals, you will embark on new beginnings.

Acceptance opens the door to self-love too. Most importantly, practicing acceptance reveals the truth that you must give yourself the utmost importance; no matter what the world has been expecting from you, no matter what's happening in the world around you.

This is what you will learn while practicing Ukeireru in your life. For me, finding my inner calm starts with the art of acceptance. What about you?

# Finding the Beauty in Imperfection with Wabi-Sabi

The very essence of my existence
Lies in the imperfections
That I embrace as my gifts from the universe.

Suppose you see a bird hurting a tree, and after it flies away, you discover the wounds carved in the body of the tree. What happens next morning? Does the tree stop flowering? No, it doesn't. Rather, the morning sunshine falls on the wounds to reflect its scars as the song of forgiveness. The tree forgives the bird, forgets yesterday's hurts, and gifts the earth a new bunch of flowers. This time, dancing with the breeze, the tree looks more beautiful because its imperfections make it stand tall among the other neighboring trees, wearing a victorious smile of pride.

This is what happens when you embrace your flaws and imperfections – you value your wounds and honor your scars that sing the story of a wondrous soul that is now transforming into an embodiment of beauty.

Sometimes, it hurts to accept your flaws and find glory in your imperfections; yet, this wonderful art helps you to cultivate the first seed of self-love. This is what you can do if you practice

Wabi-Sabi (pronounced *wah-bee-sah-bee*), a Japanese philosophy in which we can learn how to find beauty in imperfection by nurturing simplicity and the universal cycle of life.

Embracing the imperfections in the Wabi-Sabi way means you are surrendering yourself to the rhythm of seasons, nurturing the wisdom hidden in simplicity and accepting your flawed beauty. Doesn't it sound like a blissful thought where you allow yourself to align with the natural harmony?

~

It is said that with time, every wound heals, and this is never possible if you are unable to accept your brokenness and embrace your imperfections. Just think for once, how will you look without any flaws? I am sure you will look beyond beautiful. Now, think about embracing your flaws and imperfections like they are precious parts of your whole being. Think again. This time, you will look even more beautiful, for you have found the beauty in your imperfections

With your imperfections, you will be shining like the moon, and your flaws will sparkle your magic, just like the shimmering stars at night. With the help of this beautiful art, you will start embracing your flaws, and with time, you will embrace the beauty in your imperfections.

If you want to practice Wabi-Sabi in your everyday life, first, be realistic and grow a positive mindset to welcome your imperfections. You must focus on finding beauty in simplicity. Appreciate everything in its natural simplicity, accept the changes you have been experiencing, and don't forget to appreciate the uniqueness of everything when they are in their purest forms. Rather than striving for perfection, allow yourself to welcome and embrace imperfections with an optimistic outlook.

For me, in its real essence, the art of Wabi-Sabi sings the three truths of life – transience, impermanence, and incompleteness. Nobody can achieve a life that is perfect from every perspective. Therefore, it is better to accept your life with all its imperfections. Try to make your flaws your medium of change, so that you can bring transformation in your life.

Changing for the better is always a good idea. Whether it is for your everyday life routines or your healthy lifestyle, you can always embrace changes so that you can transform yourself into the best version.

This is how I practice Wabi-Sabi in my daily life. I know there are many flaws in me, but I do not try to fix the flaws that are beyond my control. Rather, I focus on the flaws that can be changed for my self-improvement and the betterment of my life. When it comes to embracing my imperfections, I recall the art of Wabi-Sabi, and I try to find beauty in my imperfections.

This is a wonderful art in which I discover the hidden truths of myself. The more I find beauty in my flaws and imperfections, the more I find new ways to explore my inner self, and this is how I make myself an epitome of beauty and grace.

What about you? Do you practice Wabi-Sabi in your life too?

# CHAPTER EIGHT

# Finding Strength in Brokenness with Kintsugi

I embrace my wounds and scars
For they make me shine like the stars.
Surrounding me with a saintly aura
They guide me to the light of wisdom
by turning my pain into a lotus.

For the last few years, I have been introspecting my brokenness, and in this process, I have discovered many truths that introduced a new version of myself to me. I found that my brokenness is an inevitable part of my wholeness; without being broken and shattered, I never realized what it means to be whole.

"*Within the depth of my brokenness, I found a surprising connection with the universe.*"

Kintsugi (pronounced *kin-tsoo-gee*) is the Japanese art of fixing broken things beautifully. What I liked the most in the art of Kintsugi is to give importance to the broken things. In life, most of us have a habit of decluttering the broken things right away from our attention, so that we do not need to see them ever again.

But what about your broken heart? Your broken soul? Or, the brokenness that you have been carrying within? In every step, in every moment?

Walking on the path of healing, at a point, you realize, this brokenness is an inseparable part of your wholeness. To become whole again, you need to embrace your brokenness as your strength, and within this brokenness, you allow enter light to heal your scars and wounds.

Here is the magic that is called Kintsugi which is all about finding beauty in the brokenness, accepting it as it is, embracing it as a precious part of yourself, and wearing it as your glorious crown.

And within this process, you heal.

In its true essence, Kintsugi is a popular art form in Japan where people preserve broken pieces of pottery and put them back with gold. An art of restoring broken pieces with shimmering gold, Kintsugi is an inner work that paves the path towards self-acceptance and emotional healing.

This is an idea of embracing brokenness so that you can accept it as a part of your wholeness. The gold that joins two broken pieces together symbolizes that you can look more beautiful with your flaws and imperfections, you can be stronger with your brokenness in the soul, and you will be shining like the moon which is an epitome of grace.

Nurturing self-compassion in the Kintsugi way helps you look within and accept your brokenness as a tool to emerge into a new version of yourself.

If you can't value and respect your brokenness, how would you expect the world to do it for you? To heal from within, at first, you need to collect your broken pieces lying shattered on the floor. Then, you need to join them with something that shows your true potential and makes you shine!

Kintsugi is a reminder to stay optimistic about the mess and chaos in life - that no matter how many missteps you have taken, at the right moment, they will fall into place, and within the process of becoming, you find calm. It is a reminder for you that healing needs time because, in each fragment of the broken parts, you are introduced to a new revelation about yourself.

Kintsugi sheds light on the truth that during the process of repairing the broken pieces, you create a new self that shines with your uniqueness – your most resilient self that shows the power of endurance and how beautifully it has transformed you into the masterpiece created with the utmost perseverance. It also acts as a metaphor to teach us the meaning and significance of accepting brokenness and turning our scars into our strength, which eventually helps in our healing process.

~

Within the process of finding strength in my brokenness and healing myself, I created a new self, and I found that this self of me is more beautiful than my previous self, because it is born with resilience and perseverance. The light entered the depths of my soul and introduced the blissful truths from where I gathered the wisdom of enlightenment.

How do you find the glory within your brokenness?

# CHAPTER NINE

# Practicing Gratitude with Kansha

I appreciate you
I appreciate me
I appreciate everyone and everything
That is part of my life.
I am grateful for having them
as they contribute to
my existence,
my joy of being,
And the process of my becoming.

While working on this book, I came across a beautiful Japanese word, Kansha (pronounced *kahn-shah*), which means thanks, gratitude, or appreciation. This single word changed my perspective toward the gratitude journaling ritual.

Before learning about Kansha, I simply wrote in my journal the things, the people, and the moments that offered me a sense of fulfillment, thus I practiced fostering a habit of showing gratitude. Being grateful for every little big thing and every instance that brings me joy, I counted them as my blessings. I wrote about them in my journal, as well as remembering and thanking the people who stood by my side through thick and thin, thus making my life a delightful ride.

But when I learned about the Kansha way of gratitude, it opened a door in me to a deeper level of understanding and realization of this word. When I utter the word 'Gratitude' for something or someone, now, it offers me a sense of humbleness and thankfulness, and a blissful aura surrounds me within these moments of calm. I discover that when I acknowledge something or someone and their contribution to my life and appreciate them in every true sense, I find contentment in the appreciation.

I pondered upon the metaphorical interpretation of Kansha and tried to practice journaling to cultivate sincere gratitude by conveying a message of appreciation. Although at the beginning, I felt it difficult to embrace my life as a whole, nurturing Kansha as a ritual of practicing Kintsugi, and accepting my life, my being as a whole, appreciating both, the good and the bad.

On this note, I remembered the word Komorebi, which means Sunlight filtering through trees. I believe life is an interplay between darkness and light, and we need to choose carefully what to look into the depth of the soul.

Thus, when I put thing thought into my gratitude journaling ritual with Kansha, it helped me focus on the good part of everything wherein learning something meaningful from the bad, and thus, I kept going through the challenges wearing the crown of victory.

When it comes to practicing gratitude journaling, I have witnessed its miraculous effects on my mind, my life, and the vibes I carry around me. I prefer to sit in my room alone while journaling. Before I start writing in my journal, I burn an incense stick or scented candle or simply spray a few puffs of the room freshener and inhale their sweet aroma. This instantly calms down my mind and uplifts my mood, no matter how stressed or worried I am. Then, I take time to ground myself and breathe slowly to embrace the stillness. I never rush while journaling; rather, I slow down and savor the slow pace of my life in those few hours when I am unfurling myself to the most beloved person on this earth - my inner self – with love and compassion.

This way, my gratitude journaling process begins with an introspective conversation with my inner self, sometimes with my inner guide. I keep writing the words in the most non-judgemental place on earth – my journal. Thus, I create a safe and comfortable space within the pages, and slowly, I start sharing my gratitude through notes of appreciation.

When it comes to writing my gratitude notes, my gratitude practice always begins with a note to Mother Earth. Writing down my message of thankfulness, I write a note to myself. After these two steps, I finally start counting my blessings. Being a spiritually inclined person and a meditation practitioner, I also acknowledge and thank the universe and the Divine Power in the form of conversation written in my journal.

Through the gratitude journaling practice, I have experienced calm and contentment because it helped me find a sense of order, address my conflicts, and process my emotions by expressing my chaotic thoughts in the form of notes, letters, and messages to my inner self. Thus, it helped me clarify my vision, reframe my thoughts, and build awareness. It significantly impacted in improving my mental, emotional, and spiritual well-being.

Thus, the art of gratitude journaling turns into a reflective, introspective, contemplative, and mindful practice that keeps bringing me the gifts and blessings of staying alive after living on the other side of life.

Have you practiced gratitude journaling yet? How about doing it in the Kansha way?

# CHAPTER TEN

# Practicing Compassion with Omoiyari

Holding the candle of compassion
I light
The path towards enlightenment.

While passing through the phase of despair and grief, I discovered the amazing power of empathy, kindness, and compassion. Being compassionate does not only help in seeing the world from a new perspective but also helps in healing your pain. You heal yourself by healing others, and this healing is not about being compassionate for someone and expecting something in return. This healing is all about healing your inner self, by stretching your hands towards the one who needs a touch of compassion.

This is what I learned from Omoiyari, the art that teaches us how selfless compassion helps in our healing process.

Omoiyari (pronounced *oh-moy-ah-ree*) is a Japanese culture of reaching out to those who need you the most at this moment. When you hold their hands to help them come out from the crisis, you find contentment in living a purposeful life. If you can learn the art of being compassionate to others by feeling their pain or sorrow or grief, or mindfully observing what they need at this right moment, you can act according to the situation, and thus, it will make them feel valued, they will know that someone cares for them from the bottom of heart. By doing this, they will be happier and more comfortable with time, and seeing them happy, your heart will be filled with happiness, too.

Omoiyari teaches us how being compassionate selflessly can make you learn others' perspectives and anticipate their needs. If you can help them out, then you can embrace happiness within.

This is a deep concept of life. Many people do not pay attention to others' needs and always love to focus on their own needs and fulfill their own wishes. But think for once, what is life if you can't hold others' hands when they need you the most? Omoiyari teaches us the vital lessons of compassion to show some care and consideration to the ones who are deprived of them at this moment.

Cultivating compassion is the first step to practicing Omoiyari in daily life. In addition, you must develop the habit of active listening and anticipating others' needs by acting with empathy and kindness without any expectation. Also, consciously choose your words and actions, and be mindful of your behavior with others. Essentially, to practice the art of compassion, you must understand others' perspectives by nurturing a compassionate heart so you can realize their situations. Not only by offering help to people who are in need, but also by understanding and realizing their needs to the core so you can take the necessary steps to make them feel comfortable, valued, and cared for.

Bringing joy and happiness to your own life is great, but when you hold the hands of others and guide them towards their paths of joy and happiness, help them recover from distress or help them to get rid of the situation they have been going through currently, is how you practice compassion for others. Meanwhile, when you heal others with compassion, gradually, you heal yourself too.

Doing something for others selflessly offers you a chance to live with a purpose and meaning in life. Here lies the secret to finding happiness within, and this truth was revealed to me when I learned about Omoiyari.

How beautiful does the concept of selfless compassion seem to you? When you delve deeper, you will come to know that Omoiyari tells us the secret of living life with the art of giving. Giving to others, giving to yourself. Cultivating compassion for others, and also, being compassionate to yourself.

If you can give your love and kindness to the ones who need it, with your empathy and compassion, you will find happiness even in the smallest things that can bring unbound joy. Because this is how you step towards making a difference and are introduced to the beauty of life.

I have started walking on this path. Would you like to join me?

# CHAPTER ELEVEN

# Perceiving the World Around with Nunchi

Before I take the step
I perceive
to conceive the idea
of how and where to put my feet next.

If you can perceive the world around you before getting trapped in the negativities spread by toxic people from your circle, wouldn't it help you stay calm and stress-free?

Thus, perceiving the world is necessary to maintain your peace of mind, and this is when you need Nunchi, the art that teaches the importance of using your emotional intelligence to perceive your circle or the people you meet every day.

It is said that if you succeed in learning Nunchi (pronounced *noon-chee*), then you will be more aware of the things you are hearing from people, than the things you are telling to them. If you listen to them more and observe their activities more than you speak your heart randomly out, then it will be better for your future interactions.

Nunchi is a Korean Philosophy. It helps to hone your emotional well-being by giving you a chance to act according to the situation. It is a great way to maintain your emotional well-being as you will act the same way you see people from your circle or people around you act with you, and as a result, you act according to their moods so you can stay away from negative vibes.

In this way, you can easily avoid any unpredictable or unacceptable situations that might feel not welcoming to you. It also helps to perceive interpersonal relationships and maintain a healthy relationship with everyone in your life.

Nunchi is a beautiful art of perceiving the world. It's a profound way in which you can look at your life and measure the depth of your emotional intelligence. The more you learn to act likewise the world acts with you, the more you can learn and behave in the Nunchi way, and the more there will be peace with others - this is how you will achieve success and happiness in your life.

To practice Nunchi in your daily life, first, you must empty your mind. Breathe, be still, and give yourself some time to understand everything around you. Don't rush, slow down. Next, mindfully observe your presence in the place you are currently in, and then, observe the presence of people around you. Next, try to interpret their intentions and measure everything with awareness.

> *"Nunchi is all about getting a quick idea of the world around you.*"

Though I am a quiet person, sometimes I react unpredictably and when everything is over, I start regretting my prompt reaction.

This is why I am trying to learn and practice Nunchi to avoid any kind of impulsive action by me.

You can also try to solve your anger issues or manage your circle. Try to give a quick Nunchi look at the world around you. Who can say, you will become more compassionate and accepting by practicing Nunchi in your everyday life?

# CHAPTER TWELVE

# Contemplating the Pause with Ikebana

What I left unheard,
The flowers whispered to my ears.

Flowers are great resources for calm and happiness. Simply watching the sight of flowers dwindling in the trees offers peace of mind to us. Their colors, patterns, textures, fragrance – everything brings us so much joy! Nurturing a flowering tree means we are nurturing our inner self to connect with nature's most beautiful gift.

This is what happens when you practice flowering arrangements with the art of Ikebana (pronounced *ike·ba·na*). Ikebana is a Japanese tradition of flower arrangements where we nurture the art of making flowers alive. It is an art to cherish mental peace in a meditative way by arranging flowers and giving life to flowers, expressing beauty, and connecting with nature.

This may sound similar to arranging flowers on a vase which we do regularly. However, Ikebana is not simply decorating your home with flowers but an artistic meditation where you nurture the flowers and cherish a connection with beauty by selecting the leaves that complement the flowers gorgeously. Therefore, it is more about the art of spending time with flowers and sculpting with them in the most beautiful combination of the leaves and branches.

Three basic rules of Ikebana should be kept in mind while practicing this art. Shin, which represents heaven, is the main element that should be placed in the center. You should keep in mind that the length must be taller than the flower vase. Soe, which symbolizes the earth, is the supporting element and it must be two-thirds the length of the Shin, and Hikae, which symbolizes humanity, is the third element that should be half of the length of the Shin.

For the Ikebana flower arrangements, flowers are intentionally arranged asymmetrically to honor the irregularities and imperfections found in nature. Thus, it also teaches you to celebrate yourself most naturally!

When you spend time arranging flowers, it seems like a mindful practice. Your focus is centered on the arranging process, and you feel the inner joy of being with flowers. Moreover, you cherish the blissful moments of smelling the flowers, appreciating their beauty, and thus bringing all your attention to the process. This tradition also helps you declutter the burdening thoughts and practice present-moment awareness. Through this meditative practice, you are introduced to the tranquil nature of the mind, and slowly, it will help in emotional release and healing while using silence as a tool to breathe.

The art of Ikebana teaches us the essential truths of cherishing the everyday moments and simplicity of life, appreciating nature and its gifts, and giving value to peace. This beautiful art helps us remember the truths of life's forgotten gifts for which we should be grateful. It also acts as a reminder of finding peace while slowing down.

Thus, engaging yourself in the art of Ikebana could be an enriching meditative process, and within that process, you rediscover the truth that to pursue happiness in everyday life, you need to embrace simple living because you don't need much to feel at peace. Pausing the constant fight within your mind and body, engaging in this art of Ikebana, offers you calm and contentment, which eventually helps your spiritual well-being.

While arranging the flowers, within that contemplative and introspective pause, you may feel they send you a message of balance and harmony. Can you hear it?

# CHAPTER THIRTEEN

# Finding a Glimpse of Yourself with Meraki

I create
To invite peace
And to offer a piece
of myself
Stealing from the 'I'
and keeping in the art
That is a reflection of mine.

When you create, you give life to something. Through the medium of creativity, you connect with your inner self – the self that remains hidden beneath the skin. But when you indulge in some form of creativity, you nurture a compassionate bond with your inner self because you go to the deepest layer of your soul where the purest truths await to be revealed.

This is what happens when you explore yourself in the Meraki way – putting your heart and soul into something with your passion, absolute devotion, and unwavering attention.

Meraki (pronounced *may-rah-kee*) is a Greek word that is used when people want to express their love for doing something with passion. Meraki holds a mirror in front of you and when you look at the reflection, you discover some hidden truths about yourself.

Meraki offers you the moments of the blissful union with your inner self.

When you embark on the pursuit of self-discovery through the art of creation, doing something with a strong passion, and dedicating your soul to the work that brings you the utmost contentment, doesn't it offer you the most gracious moments in life? You find calm amid chaos, you nurture a sense of purpose, and in the creation, you see a glimpse of your inner self that reveals to you the secrets of your uniqueness.

~

When I ask myself what is the thing that I love to do, fearlessly, boundlessly, without thinking twice about the future and enjoying being with myself?

I find two answers. One is writing, and another is singing. While writing a thoughtful piece, allowing myself to fly in the sky of imagination and going beyond the horizon where dreams meet reality, I discover my wings which give me strength and courage. While singing, I go beyond the depths of my soul and sink deep into the furthest of my soul's hidden corners.

In these moments of soul-searching through creativity, I find a glimpse of myself. That hidden me, that old me, that new me. Thus, while indulging in a form of creativity, I feel liberated.

When you do something with your heart and soul, and add a dash of creativity to the work with love, you are putting a part of yourself into it - and this is Meraki. In a deeper sense, Meraki is finding the essence of ourselves within the piece you create, whether it is creating a piece of art or craft, gardening, cooking, singing, dancing, reciting, or playing an instrument. It could also be simply decorating your dinner table or the room with flowers and other beautiful things.

Doing things with the Meraki approach can help you release negative vibes like stress and anxiety. Between your stressful work schedules, if you find a moment to do the thing you love, you will be able to welcome some moments of calm because you are doing the thing you love. This habit helps to release and reduce stress. Moreover, you give your mind the much-needed rest while exploring yourself through some form of creativity.

The same can happen while having anxious thoughts. If you can sit to make a piece of art, your mind will slowly calm down and your anxious thoughts will stop wandering as you will focus on the thing you love to do. Meraki also helps in practicing present-moment awareness by bringing your focus to your creative pursuit.

Doing things in the Meraki way means you are allowing yourself to accept the changes in your life. This, in turn, helps you to accept the new version of yourself as you will find a glimpse of the hidden self of you while nurturing your Meraki love.

I believe, nurturing my Meraki will unfold the hidden gems within this soul someday.

What about you?

# CHAPTER FOURTEEN

# Getting into self-improvement with Kaizen

The furthest corner of this universe
that remains untouched
is secretly waiting in your soul, in your heart
Where you have to keep working forever
Improving towards the better
And walking toward improvement
To keep the promise
That you have made to yourself.

When you plant a seed and nurture it every day with the utmost love and care, you witness its growth. Every day, the seed steps towards growth with small steps. Doesn't it feel peaceful to see a plant growing? From the moment of sprouting to growing taller to giving birth to a new life, witnessing the growth of the tree reminds you of the truth that slow and steady micro steps take you to the path of self-improvement. You realize the changes every day, and thus, you take one step closer to transformation.

This is how Kaizen teaches us the importance of growth and transformation through small yet constant steps.

For the last few years, I have spent quality time with myself, sitting in silence, introspecting my inner self, and contemplating the echoes that come from within. I have developed a habit of writing down in my diary the areas where I need to improve, whether it is my professional development or personal development. When I came to know about Kaizen - the beautiful idea of self-improvement, I found it very interesting.

Kaizen (pronounced *kahy-zen*) is a Japanese word that translates into the meaning of changing for the better. Kai translates as good and Zen translates as change; thus, it cumulatively translates as changing for the better self.

Kaizen is a process of self-improvement that happens within your body, mind, and soul. Constant growth in this process offers better physical health, boosts mental and emotional well-being, and gives you a chance to work toward spiritual wellness. The main goal of Kaizen is to realize your highest potential.

In a deeper sense, Kaizen is walking on the path of continuous self-development. The purpose of Kaizen is to unlock the key to your self-improvement by nurturing a positive and growth mindset, building sustainable habits, boosting emotional resilience, and encouraging self-care in your daily routine.

Suppose you are stuck at something for a long time. You have been planning to do the job for a while yet couldn't manage to finally begin doing it. At this point, taking the first step in the process seems like the most difficult job. In such moments, all you need to do is follow the Kaizen way to press the start button!

If you want to follow the process of Kaizen and improve yourself in the Kaizen way, taking one small change at a time will be helpful to have the best outcome of this process of self-improvement. With small steps, you can sustain a continuous and long-term goal of improving yourself. When you embark upon a transformation journey, if you can take one small change at a time, one day, you will certainly reach your bigger goal.

To put Kaizen into practice for self-improvement and personal development, it is better to plan a vision board and road map for your self-improvement process. First, identify your areas for improvement. Then, make the road map and vision board with your vision and mission to attain this goal. Adopt a growth and positive mindset before you start integrating the Kaizen process into your daily routine.

After identifying the easiest and simplest task to begin the process, keep working constantly according to your road map by executing baby steps. Focus on making small yet constant changes to achieve a realistic and achievable goal. Develop healthy habits to embrace change for your overall betterment.

Taking baby steps to achieve success in your self-improvement and personal development journey helps in getting significant and impactful results. However, you must keep track of your progress and reflect on your continuous transformation.

The motto is to get better each day by embracing small and actionable steps to make the change. Therefore, breaking down large goals into tiny and manageable steps will be more impactful than aiming for a drastic change overnight.

When you are following Kaizen, remember to focus on the *process* rather than achieving *perfection* in the outcome. Through regular evaluation of your daily progress, keep identifying what's working and what you need to change or replace. Constant evaluation of your progress and adjusting your approach according to the evaluation is a necessary thing in the Kaizen process. Don't bother about your mistakes, rather, look at them as learning opportunities.

For your physical well-being, grow a habit of daily walking for at least 10-15 minutes. You can gradually increase the duration. To increase productivity, you can dedicate 5-10 minutes every morning to plan your day's tasks and recognize your areas of improvement. You can also give some time for upskilling.

For your mental and emotional well-being, you can incorporate short meditation techniques or simply spend some time sitting in quietude and engaging in some breathing techniques.

I practice Kaizen with a focus on two factors: The 1% rule and Manifestation.

At first, I sit for introspection and try to reach the root of my self-improvement and personal development process. I observe my own behaviors and situations to identify the key areas where I need to prioritize my efforts. Then, I focus on taking micro steps to strive better in my life by incorporating the 1% rule of change to experience a continual and incremental improvement in my overall well-being.

The next factor in my Kaizen process is Manifestation. Kaizen is all about embracing the small changes constantly for overall betterment. Instead of waiting for radical changes to happen overnight, manifesting each sign of transformation makes Kaizen an effective approach. Manifestation proves to be an impactful approach that helps me in tracing constant transformation in my self-improvement process.

Every achievement deserves a celebration. Whether it's small or huge, every minor or major improvement should be celebrated.

So, along the way of self-improvement and personal development, acknowledge every success and celebrate them in your own way.

I have been practicing Kaizen for the last few years, but I have given less attention to my professional skills than my mental and emotional well-being. This is why I believe, now it's time to improve my professional skills. I am planning to introspect myself to address the areas of improvement and then work on them following the 1% rule and manifestation approach. I am also planning to focus on my spiritual well-being in the Kaizen way.

What are you planning to practice Kaizen in your life?

# CHAPTER FIFTEEN

# Finding Happiness at the Job with Arbejdsglæde

I work to celebrate my survival
I work to celebrate my existence.
By doing what I love
I work to celebrate my aliveness.

We work to earn and improve our lifestyle, and we consider it a source of happiness. Earning for the bread and butter seems like the best resource of happiness in life, isn't it? But what about the stressful work hours, consistent meetings, hectic job schedules, and constant pressure to meet the deadlines?

All these factors play a significant role in our workplace and thus, it seems difficult to find happiness while working as we are most stressed at our workplace and keep searching for a way to nurture a healthy atmosphere at work that would benefit our overall well-being.

This is why we need to pursue Arbejdsglæde – happiness at work. Doesn't it sound like a wonderful idea that helps us receive peace of mind? Arbejdsglæde (pronounced *ah-bite-sgleh-the*) is a Scandinavian concept that is aimed at gifting our moments of happiness while working. It is an essential art that helps us reduce our stress and anxiety at the workplace because you work with intrinsic joy.

During my research for this series, I was introduced to many blissful arts of life that surprised me, and I pondered upon the thought of how I could incorporate these beautiful concepts into my everyday life to find calm and contentment.

One of the thoughts that kept me thinking deeply about my work and my chosen career field, was that one day, I came across the blissful concept that teaches us how to celebrate happiness at work. The Danish people call this Arbejdsglæde. Happiness at work seems quite an impossible task for everyone. But not for people who find happiness at work in the Arbejdsglæde way!

If you can incorporate this art into your daily life, you will enjoy your work as much as you enjoy a vacation. When translated, the term Arbejdsglæde means to find the joy of working. Along with this, it also aims to find good vibes and high energy in your workplace. Therefore, it is all about looking forward to being content at work and achieving success in your career.

Finding happiness at work means enjoying your work, and it only happens when you are passionate about your work. If you choose your work field considering your love and passion, then it will be easier to be happy while working because you are doing what you love to do.

It is easier than it sounds. If you want to practice Arbejdsglæde, first, you need to ask yourself a few questions:

1. What work do I like to do?
2. Am I passionate about this?
3. What are the reasons that make me deliver my best to my workplace?
4. What keeps me going at my work every day?
5. Is it the work that helps to balance my work and family?

If your answer to all the above questions is Yes, then it is your dream job where you will certainly find happiness. But if you see any of your answers as No, then you need to think about your work field twice.

Following the Arbejdsglæde way at your work offers you a sense of fulfillment and contentment at work, which eventually helps you work with peace of mind by nurturing a positive emotional environment at your job. As a result, you can nurture more creativity, come up with new ideas, learn new skills, have more energy, and feel motivated to work with more passion.

It is said that if you find happiness, it is good, but if you do not, you must create it. The same goes for the art of life that comes to gift you happiness at work. With the concept of Arbejdsglæde, you will come to know what you love to do.

If you are not happy while working in your current job, then it is time to find what you love to do. Because this is the only way you will find happiness while working.

I know which work makes me happy. Do you know about yours?

# CHAPTER SIXTEEN

# Taking a Break from Work with Fika

I pause to savor the moment
I pause to ponder upon my experience.
When I ponder upon my life
It comes to meet me in fragments.

There is a secret to enjoying your work. Do you know how? Well, that's a secret!

So, Fika is the beautiful art that reveals this secret to us. You can work yet enjoy the working hours by taking small breaks with Fika.

In the Swedish Fika ritual, people love to gather for a small break from their work which helps them work with a peaceful mind. While having a Fika break, you can eat snacks and drink coffee to savor every bit of the pause. You can also enjoy chatting with your friends or colleagues. Thus, Fika becomes a welcoming tradition practiced in the workplace to work with more clarity and vision because you work with a calm mind.

In Sweden, it is a nice tradition to have a small break during the long hours of work and enjoy the breaks by munching cakes and snacks and sipping on their favorite beverages.

The origin of the word Fika (pronounced *fee-kuh*) is a 19th-century word *kaffi* that when inverted, is derived as Fika. Fika is a popular Swedish word translated as drinking coffee while munching sweet treats. People also enjoy chatting with their friends and colleagues during their Fika break and it acts as a moment of refreshment in the middle of the long working hours.

Although Fika means a coffee and cake break in the middle of your work, however, this is much more than only taking a break. Fika is a nice art of taking and savoring the intentional break. It is a blissful concept that offers you a chance to cultivate healthy communication with your colleagues.

By nurturing this peaceful practice of utilizing the coffee break time, you can find a momentary escape from the workload, which in turn, helps you savor the pause, and relieve your mind.

While working at the office, many times people feel monotonous for the consistent work assignments. As a result, they feel bored, and thus, their productivity can lessen significantly. But, instead of working continuously, if they can take small breaks and enjoy their breaks munching sweet snacks and having light talks with colleagues, it will refresh their moods. As a result, they will get back their energy to work more.

To practice Fika, first, you need to set a dedicated time when you can get a mindful break from your work. Prepare your favorite beverage and bring your favorite snacks. Find a quiet and comfortable corner and start engaging in a conversation with your friends and colleagues.

If you want to enjoy your Fika hour alone, then engage in a conversation with your inner self or simply savor the break time with relaxing vibes. Fika is a mindful practice that helps your well-being by offering you some time to rest your mind and body. You must remember that during your Fika hour, you need not rush, instead, give your Fika hour all the love and time it deserves.

Although one of the key aspects of the Fika ritual is social interaction while enjoying the beverage and snacks, if you are a remote employee or freelancer and don't have anyone to join in your Fika ritual, practicing Fika alone is fine. Therefore, integrating a Fika hour can be followed in remote work set-up too. If you don't have any colleagues to have a chat with, don't worry. You can practice Fika alone, by taking a small break from work, sitting some time in an idle mode, sipping in your cup of coffee, having snacks on your plate, and enjoying the moments of solitude. It is all about savoring your pause while practicing self-care and self-love.

The Fika ritual is also helpful to avoid burnout at work. Taking a small break from the hectic schedule at work offers you a chance to celebrate the momentary bliss. But make sure whenever you opt for Fika, you need to be slow and savor the pause without any rush. This way, you will feel refreshed and rejuvenated when you return to work after your Fika ritual. Therefore, Fika simply acts like the much-needed escape to rewire your brain and reset your mind with peace and calm.

Well, my coffee is ready, and I am going to take a Fika break from my work. I will have some cookies while reading a book. Thus, I am going to take a break from work and enjoy my Fika ritual.

Would you like to join me? Come, let's have our Fika hour together!

# Giving Value to Your Leisure Time with Susegad

Sitting quiet
Embracing the stillness
I savor the pause.
I breathe
and let this moment be my favorite muse.

When I want some time for relaxation, I say, "It's enough, now it's time for some leisure activities." But what do the Goan people say when they need their leisure time for relaxation? Well, they would like to say in Konkani, '*Maka suseg di*', which means give me peace or quietness.

Susegad (pronounced *soo-seh-gahd*) is a Konkani word that means to feel content and fulfilled through various activities of relaxation. In Goan culture, Susegad is how the Goan people find peace of mind through relaxation. Susegad comes from 'sossegado', a Portuguese word that means quiet. Thus, this Goan culture of Susegad, where people love to celebrate life with some quiet and peaceful moments, is born.

In our hectic schedule, we find very little time to give our minds a chance to relax. We are prone to work, work, and work more. Our minds often keep working even while we are inactive or sleeping, and this remains unknown to us. As a result, the restless mind becomes exhausted and it affects your mental health. This is a strange fact that made me ponder upon my lifestyle – how much we stress our mind that it keeps working even when we are not actively doing something. I also discovered that I keep tracking my to-do list all the time, sometimes even while going to sleep. I am always counting my tasks ticked off and keep checking the tasks that I am yet to finish. This way, my mind is occupied with some thoughts all the time.

But very recently, I realized that giving value and importance to your relaxation time or leisure time is equally important to giving priority to your work. Now, I prioritize investing time in relaxing my mind and body to prevent burnout. We often ignore the signs of burnout even when we know that we have been feeling overstressed at work. This is why, following the Susegad way of life offers a chance to allow yourself the time to pause and slow down. It's all about enjoying your slow pace of life, savoring the moments to rest your mind, and within these moments of self-love, self-care, and mindfulness, pursuing calm and contentment.

During my research work for this book, when I came across the Susegad way of life, I found it very interesting. Susegad acts like a reminder that no matter where you live in the world, you can add sprinkles of magic to your monotonous life by making relaxing rituals an integral part of life.

Susegad teaches us that we should give equal importance to our leisurely activities in the same way we prioritize our work. Therefore, if you want to practice Susegad, you need to be guilt-free about your leisure time, rather, you must savor your leisurely hours and indulge yourself in some relaxation activities. After finishing a tedious job, all you need is some moments of relief and rest. You can go on a vacation, watch a movie, read books, listen to music, or simply sit in nature. You can go for a trip to the woods, spend some peaceful moments there, and sleep amidst the lush greenery. Or, you can have exquisite cuisine and give yourself a treat with delicious food.

Following the Susegad way, you find a momentary escape from your monotony. Susegad tells us how to create healthy habits and lifestyle routines that can lend us some moments of happiness and peace.

In its true essence, Susegad is a wonderful way to find the sweetness of everything that comes your way. It reminds you that life could be lived at a slow pace and enjoying your leisure time. Thus, you find calm and contentment in the present moment and celebrate the relaxing hours with full awareness.

It's been a while since I am working on this book. I think it's my time for some rest and relax. So, I am going to find my Susegad rituals and enjoy the leisurely hours without any guilt. I am planning some self-care activities to add more fun to my Susegad.

Would you like to join me?

# CHAPTER EIGHTEEN

# Turning the Online Mode Off with Koselig

Winter is the time
for waking up from the slumber,
and savoring the moments of warmth
in the brace of peace that feels like home.

Think of the blissful cocoon – the place you enter before the approaching winter, and enjoy the little things to celebrate this period of hibernation with simple living. When the oppressive darkness surrounds the earth, the weather becomes gloomy and you search for light and optimism, practice Koselig – the art of cherishing ordinary and simple things to embrace the warmth in coziness.

If you are wondering about the art that will help you to enjoy every bit of cosiness, and find happiness within that contentment and peace, then it is time to have some time for Koselig.

People who look for happiness in the winter season may find it in a hot cup of coffee or the warmth of their blanket. It is nice to find pleasure in these little moments of coziness, and this is how Koselig teaches us to embrace calm and contentment while enjoying our blissful celebration of winter!

When translated, the Norwegian word Koselig (pronounced *koo-sh-lee*) can be interpreted as a shared and safe sense of togetherness. In its true essence, Koselig means to find happiness that encompasses feelings of safety, warmth, and good.

When winter comes, I find immense pleasure in the warmth of a blanket, while sipping my cup of coffee and watching a movie. It is my favorite hobby during the cold winter days. I choose my favorite book, with my favorite playlist in the loop, wrapping myself in the shawl and enjoying the coziness.

However, Koselig is not only meant to find the happiness in coziness that you will find inside your house. If you are a wanderer, a nature lover, then you can find it outside too. For this purpose, you need to step out to the woods, have a bonfire or some other fireplace, and wrap your shawl to feel the warmth around your body. Therefore, enjoying winter in the Koselig way means you are embracing peace in coziness, adventures, and togetherness.

If you can burn a candle and sit around it, wrapping a shawl, with a cup of coffee and savoring every bit of the solitude, it will be your Koselig. Within that coziness, you will find contentment in the little things that offer you calmness and stillness - it is when your peace is celebrated in the Koselig way.

Practicing Koselig means pursuing calm and contentment by meditating on the little things embodying simplicity. You can meditate on your body, the flames of the burning candles, the fragrance of the candles, the warmth of the shawl, the peaceful ambiance around you, and all the little things that offer you peace.

On the winter days, I often do one thing. I frequently turn the online mode off. I like to sit under the sun, feel the natural warmth of the winter morning, and soak myself in the sun. I sit under the sun and read my favorite books. Thus, I allow the natural warmth to enter my body. This habit helps me overcome the gloom of cold wintry weather.

I even start preparing my winter reading list before the arrival of winter. I frequently take digital detox during the winter days. I go outside and sit under the sun. I love to feel the warmth of nature. Sitting quietly, feeling the sunshine on my face, I pursue my happiness in the present moment. You can also practice Koselig in this way.

When you enjoy being together with your loved ones and celebrating the happiness around them, it is also a Koselig way of happiness.

Whether you love being with people and enjoy being surrounded by your friends and family members or simply sit in a lonely corner and feel the quietude, Koselig is about finding contentment in the brace of love and light.

I have started making my Koselig plans to enjoy this winter!

Are you planning your Koselig too?

# CHAPTER NINETEEN

# Connecting to Nature with Friluftsliv

I walk bare feet
Touching the ground beneath
and thank Mother Earth
whispering in the gentle breeze
my silent prayer of gratitude.

Do you love nature? Are you passionate about going out in nature? I think many of us feel desperate to step out of home when we work for long or spend the whole day inside our homes.

When we feel we can't breathe more inside these claustrophobic places, whether it's our home or our workplace, we want to go to open air - and that is what the art of Friluftsliv helps us nurturing the practice of going to nature and enjoying the time spending in open air.

The Norwegian concept of Friluftsliv (pronounced *Free-Loofs-Leaf*) is described as 'open-air living'. If you want to live your life in the Friluftsliv way, then you need to go outside of your home and live the outdoor life to its fullest.

In the Scandinavian culture, Friluftsliv is a beautiful way to enjoy open-air living. It's a part of their lives so that they can see the greenery, water, forests, flowers, the sky, and everything in nature, and this way, they enjoy being in the open air and incorporate this habit into their daily life routine.

Friluftsliv is a blissful tradition that encourages us to practice slow living and foster a deeper connection with nature.

Scandinavians have a strong passion for nature and this is the heart of the art that is called Friluftsliv. This expression was very popular in the 1850s. Norwegian poet and playwright, Henrik Ibsen used this special term to bring out the value of spending time in nature. Especially when the person visits a remote place, far from the urban noise and the hustles of city life, he can explore the place and derive its essence while living in the open air. Moreover, they can uplift their moods with the soothing sound of nature. This helps in getting a better result to maintain their mental, emotional, and physical well-being.

Friluftsliv can be practiced with simple activities to enjoy nature in your small breaks. If you are at your workplace, you can take a small break at lunchtime and go outdoors. Whether it is walking on the grass, running in the forest, or watching the flowing river simply by sitting beside the river.

Many times, people enjoy being with friends and having an adventure in nature to celebrate Friluftsliv. Sometimes, they can go to a mountain hut and simply spend time being there, watching the snowfall and enjoying the chilling wind. This way, people can get a chance to go out of their workplaces and engage themselves in different outdoor activities as per their own choices.

After learning about Friluftsliv, I started visiting the nearby park every afternoon. Sitting there amidst the greenery and serenity, I embraced my stillness and the quietude to gift myself some moments of calm. Within the moments of celebrating myself amidst nature, I felt so much peace.

I often visit the nearby temple premises, where we have some cement benches built in front of the temple courtyard. After working for some days with a stressful schedule, I deliberately give myself some time to take a mindful break, walk to the temple premises, and sit on the benches alone. Quietly sitting in the lap of nature, listening to the chirping of birds, watching greenery, and smelling flowers, I find clarity of thoughts, and I discover how significantly nature helps me heal.

Being in nature helps me strengthen my mental and physical abilities in the manifold. After all, who can ignore the magical effect of going out, breathing in the open air, and soothing your eyes with the lavish greenery? Here lies the magic of spending time in nature. While practicing Friluftsliv, I try to nurture a sense of wonder and practice mindfulness through present-moment awareness. I embrace the peace in feeling oneness with nature. I realize the power of Awe most beautifully when I become one with nature, moments when I feel a soulful connection with Mother Earth.

It's already 5 PM and I am feeling very tired while working on this book. Let me have a small break from work and go for a walk in the nearby park. So, I am going to enjoy my Friluftsliv hours and celebrate a deeper connection with nature.

Have you discovered the wonders of being one with nature?

# CHAPTER TWENTY

# Traveling to the Forest with Shinrin-yoku

Into the woods,
I found someone back
Whom I had lost, long ago,
In the urban cacophony.
Bathing myself in the enchantments,
Breathing in the euphoric calmness,
I immersed in the ponderings
that slowly became a blissful symphony.

For every nature lover, forests offer a treat to the mind, body, and soul. Getting into the woods not only gives you a chance to introspect yourself in a lost-and-found way but also helps you find inner calm and contentment.

When it comes to being lost in the woods, why not know about the beautiful art of happiness that teaches us the benefits of forest bathing?

Forest Bathing, how amazing this word sounds to all nature lovers! We all keep looking for a chance relentlessly, to escape this hustle of life, go to the woods, and just breathe. This is what we can do with Shinrin-yoku.

The term Shinrin-yoku (pronounced *shin-rin-yo-ku*) emerged in Japan. In the 1980s, it was a means of physiological and psychological exercise. The word Shinrin-yoku means forest bathing or taking yourself to the forest atmosphere. However, the purpose of getting lost in the woods with the Japanese art of Shinrin-yoku is twofold. It offers you a chance to get relief from your burnout with the help of eco-therapy. In addition, Shinrin-yoku is a beautiful way to inspire you to connect to nature and cherish the peaceful ambiance of the forests.

I was born and brought up in a city where protecting the greenery was an integral part of our lives. In our city, there was a culture of planting trees, more trees, and more trees. We were never tired of planting trees; although we had more than enough, yet, we were into the habit of planting the new saplings here and there. Also, we had official rules to protect trees in our city - if anyone was caught cutting trees, then it was considered a punishable offense. That's why my childhood was spent in the lap of greenery of nature.

We had a dense forest surrounding the town alongside the gently flowing river. So, whenever we wanted to give ourselves a treat of fresh air, we used to visit the forest side or walk inside the forest, hear the sound of the forest, and smell the trees. The serenity and calmness inside the forest bathed us with a peaceful melody, which helped remove our stress and calm our minds.

After learning about Shinrin-yoku, I went to the forest situated one hour away from my home and surrendered myself to the paradise of green. It acted like an ecotherapy – moments of serenity and tranquility, meditating upon nature's treasures, walking in awe and peace, and fostering a deeper awareness of my five senses.

To practice Shirnrin-yoku, you can incorporate the art of forest bathing by taking a trip to the woods and enjoying the hours of peace by celebrating the oneness with nature. You can also practice present-moment awareness with deeper attention to all your senses. For this purpose, you need to engage your senses in watching the soothing green, listening to the sounds of the forest, inhaling the earthen smell, the fragrance of flowers, and the wooden smell of trees, tasting the sweet and sour fruits, and touching the leaves, flowers, fruits, and bodies of trees.

The art of forest bathing offers you blissful moments when you surrender yourself to the rhythm of the forest. When you are walking inside a forest, spend some unforgettable moments with wonder in your eyes and gratitude in your heart, and then, bring all your awareness to the present moment by engaging with all your senses, thus connecting with your inner self to a deeper level. Shinrin-yoku is not only a significant way to find calm and contentment, but also a mindful practice that offers you a chance for self-discovery amid the peaceful ambiance of the forest.

The greenery helps you heal. Greenery is a way to soothe your mind, body, and soul. When you step into the forests, a sense of peace and calm surrounds you. This is not only a wonderful way to get yourself lost in the woods, but also to be found yourself in a new way, amid the green.

Forest bathing is a beautiful art that offers you moments of self-discovery.

When you start practicing Shinrin-yoku, the art of forest bathing, it will reduce your mental stress to a great extent. Also, it helps in uplifting the mood and you can focus on your creative pursuit with a calm mind. Shinrin-yoku is the way to protect your peace and welcome tranquil bliss.

I am in search of the forest where I had left a part of me in my childhood. Would you like to take me with you?

Let's have a getaway to the green.

Shinrin-yoku is calling!

# Calming Down Your Anxious Mind with Mångata

I was looking at the moon,
with the clouds, floating.
For a moment, there,
I saw a glimpse of mine,
silently meditating.

The Swedish word Mångata (pronounced *mawn-gah-tah*) has its origin in the words 'mane' which means moon, and 'gate' which means road or street or path. Thus, it forms Mångata, making it a poetic word that means a moon road or a moon path. When translated into English, the word Mångata means 'the roadlike reflection of moonlight on water.'

As I learned the meaning, slowly, I fell in love with the imagery of this beautiful word portrayed in my mind - on a moonlit night, when the moon is glowing with its divine aura in the night sky, I am watching its reflection on a gently flowing stream and listening to the music of the flowing water, bathing myself in the gracious white beam of light.

In such moments, the world becomes a standstill and within this tranquility, I discover a blissful harmony with nature and my inner self.

If you practice Mångata, the tranquil moments gift you this blissful union.

Mångata tells you to find peace within the moments that you spend with the lonely moon and feel the tranquil ambiance around you. In its real essence, Mångata refers to the reflection of the moon, especially the long and glimmering reflection that we can see on a usually large body of water. When the moon reflects this way, it resembles a street that seems shining with the aura of a moonlit night.

When we are stressed or living with anxious thoughts for several days, then we need some lonely and quiet moments for self-reflection and present-moment awareness. If you can spend some time with yourself in quietude, bringing all your attention to the present moment, it offers you a sense of calm by fostering a deeper connection with your inner self. As a result, you can ponder upon the situation with a calm mind and gradually find the solutions. In addition, walking with the moon and allowing yourself to feel the blissful atmosphere helps in self-exploration which brings you some truths that act as positive affirmations.

In your pursuit of calm and contentment, practicing Mångata is a significant and profound habit that could be incorporated into your daily life. Go for a walk in the moonlit night, preferably beside a stream, and watch the reflection of the moon in the flowing stream. When you see the moon and its reflection in the river water, it offers you peace, and within this blissful serenity, you find some moments of tranquility. The soothing vibes significantly help in calming your anxious mind.

The sight of the glowing moon offers you a sense of peace and calm. Its soft light and gentle glow create a visually soothing effect in your mind, thus promoting inner calm by reducing stress and anxiety. Moreover, watching the moon or the reflection of the moon offers you relaxing vibes which is extremely helpful in calming down the restlessness within.

When I first learned about the concept of Mångata, I was moved by this concept. Now, I frequently practice this blissful ritual to calm down my mind and foster a harmonious connection with nature.

For me, sitting somewhere beside a stream or the river and watching the moon or its reflection works as a contemplative meditation when I connect with my inner self to a deeper level, ponder upon some questions that offer me moments of self-discovery, and perceive the rhythm of life to nurture a sense of harmony. I also sing while watching the moon and engage in an introspective conversation with the moon. Thus, this blissful practice plays a significant role in my spiritual well-being because, in the reflection of the moon, I see a reflection of mine, too.

It's summer here, and the full moon night is calling me for the blissful union. I am planning to go for my night walk in the garden, bare feet, touching the soft carpet of grass beneath, inhaling the sweet fragrance of the summer blossoms, and watching the silvery moon glowing with divine bliss.

When was the last time you had walked with the moon?

# CHAPTER TWENTY-TWO

# Living a Balanced Life with Lagom

This feels right
When I have enough of everything
Not too much
Not too little
But something in between
Where I find
A sense of balance, harmony, and peace.

At times, we all feel stressed while working for long hours constantly. However, if there is a concept that teaches us about living a balanced lifestyle in which we can work while enjoying our life, wouldn't it be great?

Before you search for such an art, here I present to you Lagom, the Swedish art of being more productive yet enjoying the happiest version of you. It introduces us to the way of life in which we can learn how to work not too much yet not too little; rather, work just enough.

In its real essence, Lagom is all about living a balanced life.

Workaholic people tend to work more and more, with all their focus on their work and future schedules like business meetings, client meetings, and other difficult responsibilities. However, if they can have an apt combination of work-life balance, this will secretly work towards their productivity along with developing a good relationship with their loved ones.

This Scandinavian buzzword, Lagom (pronounced *lah-gom*) is the key to opening the door towards a blissful life. Because often we feel too much stressed while working. At that moment, if we can practice this beautiful art of Lagom, we can find joy and peace in life.

Lagom means to have everything in life, yet only good enough. The origin of the word Lagom is the old Swedish word Laghum. This translates as according to law; sometimes this also translates as according to custom.

In your everyday life, you can follow Lagom by doing everything in just the right amount which is the main purpose of Lagom. This is a blissful way of life in which you can work peacefully at your workplace. While working and leveraging all your resources, you can also take small breaks. And at that time, you can strike a chord of balance between your flexibility of work; which could be attained by exploring creativity with enthusiasm. On the other hand, keep stability by focusing on your structured role at work.

To practice Lagom, you need to put 'just the right amount' of yourself into everything. For this purpose, you need to find balance in every aspect of life and deliberately avoid any kind of extremes.

In addition, you need to embrace moderation and prioritize a simple and sustainable lifestyle. For this purpose, you must include small breaks in between your work hours, declutter your space, eat a balanced and healthy diet, connect with nature, and be mindful of your daily consumption habits to maintain a balanced lifestyle.

When it comes to nurturing a Lagom lifestyle, you need to integrate this concept into every aspect of your daily routine.

For eating habits, you must eat the right amount, not too much, not too little, the exact amount you need to fulfill your appetite. Make sure you carefully avoid overindulgence, instead, focus on prioritizing fresh and seasonal produce more.

For your home, declutter the extra baggage and simplify your living space. Remove unnecessary items and focus on the things that bring you true joy. Incorporate minimalism and sustainability to make your home a perfect place for Lagom lifestyle.

For your work-life balance, you need to work only the right amount. Also, you must take small breaks from your constant and hectic schedule and enjoy your time to pause and rest. Make sure you avoid overcommitting yourself to your job, and instead, consciously rest your mind and body in between your working hours.

In addition, remember to spend time outdoors, enjoy your walks in nature, and cherish your connection with nature by decorating your living space with indoor plants and fresh flowers. You can also engage in moderate exercise and regular physical activities.

In Lagom living, you must prioritize quality over quantity because when it comes to your choice, you must do everything just in the right amount.

Most importantly, in the Lagom lifestyle, you must savor every moment and avoid rushing or procrastinating. Slow down, be mindful of your every action, and do everything with a perfect balance.

Lagom helps to lead you to a delightful life as there will be scope for living a more balanced lifestyle. Lagom also helps to reduce the environmental impact on you, and as a result, it improves your work-life balance. Lagom is an extremely helpful art to live a healthy lifestyle. If practiced at home, it also helps you follow a minimalistic and sustainable approach, which in turn, reduces stress and anxiety. Thus, Lagom profoundly contributes to your overall well-being.

But what I love the most about Lagom is its blissful offering to live a balanced life. You can cherish the calm and contentment in simple living by practicing a Lagom lifestyle. In the Lagom way of living, you will be able to work and also spend time with your loved ones which is essential to lead to a delightful and peaceful life!

Well, I think I have done just enough work for today. As of now, it is my time for Lagom. I am going to the nearby park with my mother to breathe in fresh air and cherish our moments of togetherness sitting in the lap of nature.

What about you?

# CHAPTER TWENTY-THREE

# Resting Your Mind-Body-Soul with Niksen

By doing nothing,
I do the most important thing
Because this is when I rest
my ever-wandering and ever-wondering mind.

For some days, I was determined to start working on my new project. I wrote in my journal the pending tasks and assured myself that I would start executing them one by one from the very next day. But when I started doing those things together, all the tasks jumbled up, and I got confused about where to start! In conclusion, I thought it was better to keep them unfinished and just enjoy floating on the boat of doing nothing.

At that moment, I remembered this beautiful Italian phrase: *Dolce Far Niente*, which means the sweetness of doing nothing. It could be described as 'sweet idleness'.

In Italy, people enjoy relaxing and resting their minds by doing nothing. This might sound a bit luxurious for many, but it's a wonderful art of being in a meditative state when you are doing absolutely nothing. This is an ideal art for offering your mind, body, and soul the much-needed rest by being in idleness filled with the sweetness of restfulness.

You might address it as being lazy or blame yourself for not being enough productive or creative. But the art of doing nothing is much more than sitting with idleness or avoiding any kind of activity. It's like spending your days carefree, without rushing towards your to-do list and finishing the tasks scheduled for today, and this is what we are going to talk about now – Niksen - the art of doing nothing.

Niksen (pronounced *nik-suhn*) is the Dutch concept of doing nothing and spending your leisure hours absorbing the gift of this nothingness. It's all about doing something without any predefined goal or a certain purpose; it's actually, purposefully doing nothing!

Just think for once, isn't it amazing for all of us, to have a small break from the rush of life and sit in the balcony to watch the sunset colors? Or, to walk on the grass field, just feeling the softness of the grass below your feet? Or, just lying lazily on the bed and simply doing nothing and letting the time pass?

~

Many people might think that the doing nothing concept is an act of luxury or laziness. But the truth is, this is a beautiful way to gift yourself some moments of peace and calm, without thinking about the outer world, at least for a while. Because this is all about being present in the moment and letting yourself flow in the momentary bliss.

This special state of doing nothing gives you the stillness of mind. While practicing Niksen, it feels like you are breathing out as much as breathing in.

When you have a long list of tasks scheduled, it's obvious to end up being stressed out. You will be worried about the proper execution of your tasks. Moreover, they need to be delivered by the deadline. So, these thoughts make you anxious and create an extra burden on your mind.

But, if you can find some moments when you will be doing nothing, at those moments, you will rest your mind. As a result, you will find a way to restore peace of mind and restore your energy to restart the work. A part of your brain might be still active in processing information, and it's okay if it happens. Don't rest your mind forcefully, rather, slowly float yourself to the flow of doing nothing.

If you are anxious about your pending tasks, assure yourself by saying that you are not giving up things, you are just taking a break. You are trying to balance things peacefully. This moment is all about giving yourself some rest and enjoying being in the moment. Relish yourself to relinquish your ever-wandering mind by doing nothing, and watch the magic happen in the middle of that nothingness.

This is the time for some quirky questions to life and getting their unpredictable replies.

~

Even when you are doing nothing, you are doing at least one thing. It might seem that you are just chilling and giving yourself some well-deserved me time, but it's also true that even in that nothingness, you are still active. You are doing the thing that you love to do. You are indulging in something that gives you peace and happiness, and thus, you can feel calm from within.

**And the truth is, purposefully doing nothing, you walk closer to your purpose!**

Though it looks very easy to dwell in the state of doing nothing, however, the fact is that doing nothing is an art that you need to learn. Because, when you aim to sit casually beside the window and let the world pass by, even at that time, you might have some thoughts in mind about your pending tasks, your children, your work, your life, and many more.

So, here are some ways that can help you to spend time doing nothing without any worries.

First, define your own doing-nothing mode. Everyone is different, everyone is unique. All of us define peace and calm in our own ways. So, it depends on you how would you like to define your doing nothing activity. You can read, you can write, you can sing, you can dance. You can listen to your favorite music and watch it rain, sitting beside the window. Even you can doodle or draw something without thinking about its outcome. Don't judge yourself that you're not doing something worthy or something useful. You don't need to do something productive always. Just let yourself flow with your happy pace.

Next, find where your happiness lies. The main purpose of practicing the art of doing nothing is to gift you the sweetness of nothingness. So, choose the one that gives you happiness from within. Choose a way of relaxing that offers you peace and calm. Don't be stressed out if you can't find anything suitable for your happy leisure. Just sit with a cup of coffee and listen to your favorite singer. Or have a bowl of popcorn and watch your favorite movie, forgetting how many times you have watched it before. After all, it's all about being happy by doing nothing.

Always start with small steps. At first, start with a smaller time frame. You can start with having a five-minute or ten-minute break from the daily schedule and let yourself indulge in doing nothing. Choose a time when you are less bothered with the world. Refrain from burdening your mind with unnecessary thoughts. Choose a place where you feel comfortable, and start floating into the mode of doing nothing.

Remember one thing, this doing nothing phase is all about restoring your peace of mind. So don't be hard on yourself thinking about how to relax. You can choose anything to do, you can pick something from the activities mentioned above or you can simply do nothing - just allowing yourself to rest with some moments of peace and calm.

~

When I practice the art of doing nothing with Niksen, I focus on two things: Affirming myself to just breathe and be, and mindfully slowing down. I take meaningful pause from the rush of life. I assure myself that after a tough schedule, I deserve a proper rest, and this is the time when I need to slow down.

During the Niksen hour, I disconnect myself from all the distractions and unplug myself from the world. At that time, I take a mindful pause from my daily schedule, slow down, and spend some blissful moments by doing nothing purposefully.

I try to practice Niksen daily by stretching my body, decluttering my mind, and relieving my stress for at least fifteen minutes. Sometimes, I practice Niksen while sipping my morning tea and watching the trees outside my window. One of my favorite activities is sitting on the balcony, watching my neighborhood kids playing in the afternoon, and enjoying the silent play of colors in the sunset sky.

However, while practicing the art of doing nothing, it's important to fix a specific time duration. When you are about to start your Niksen mode, you need to figure out how much time you can dedicate to this phase. Whether you choose some activities to do or you choose to do absolutely nothing and just relax, you can fix a time slot for that. It could be fifteen minutes, thirty minutes, one hour a day, or a week. Just make sure not to be hard on yourself in that duration of doing nothing phase. Be calm and let yourself flow with the sweetness of resting and rejuvenating the mind, body, and soul.

Float the boat and discover the miracles of purposefully doing nothing.

Happy Niksen to you!

# CHAPTER TWENTY-FOUR

# Surrendering Yourself to the Natural Flow with Wu Wei

*I surrender myself to the stillness
and let myself float in the river of being
To hear the answers
from the whisper of silence
and the devoid of nothingness.*

Sometimes, peace needs an invitation, and Wu Wei is that invitation to peace.

If you allow yourself to flow freely, what happens then is a miracle. If you put unnecessary effort into doing anything, many times, it gets stuck at a point, and moving on from that point becomes more difficult. On the other hand, when you do things without any external force but give them time and space to happen on their own, things happen in the same way they are meant to have happened.

When you flow like a river, aligning yourself with your nature of being, you surrender yourself to your inner guide, and then, nothing is left undone, because you are doing things in the Wu Wei way.

Wu Wei (pronounced *woo-WAY*), a concept that is celebrated in Chinese Philosophy, is an act of non-doing. When you read this for the first time, you might think that Wu Wei is all about falling into laziness or relaxing peacefully, forgetting about all your daily stress. But this would be a misinterpretation of the concept because this is a concept of life that unlocks the key to bringing out your full potential naturally.

In its true essence, Wu Wei teaches you how sometimes staying in your own motion can be extremely helpful to become the best version of yourself. Wu Wei doesn't mean sitting idle and letting things be done on their own. When you follow the Wu Wei way, it means you are allowed to do things with an effortless action.

In Daoism, 'Wu Wei' means 'non-action' or 'effortless action', which signifies the importance of following The Way. Here, the way means your free-flow activity which could be practiced by aligning your actions with your natural flow or aligning your activity with the flow of the universe, especially when you achieve a state of harmony with the universe.

Essentially, following Wu Wei means you are plugging into the 'doing nothing' mode, but this time, you may not be involved in resting your mind; rather, you are actually doing your everyday things, but you are allowing yourself to flow without forcefully interfering with your natural state.

To practice Wu Wei, you must focus on being aware and fully present in the moment. You must observe your surroundings with full awareness and be mindful of your senses. In this art of surrendering, you must let go of any external force to control the flow of your life. Rather, be attentive to act spontaneously in alignment with your natural state of being and flow of things. Floating with the stream, you must avoid forcefully taking control of the situation.

During the Wu Wei mode of non-action (or natural action), embrace the stillness and nurture the harmonious flow by doing meditation, practicing mindfulness, deep breathing exercises, and cultivating patience to allow yourself to go with the flow.

Letting the resistance go and embracing the outcomes by nurturing an unwavering faith in the universe and the Divine Force that guides you along, the art of Wu Wei allows your actions to unfold in front of you with their natural pace and flow.

*"Thus, by accepting your life's actions without any judgment, you become more thoughtful about your natural state of existence and aware of your spontaneity."*

For mindful activities, you can engage in everyday tasks where you find peace. This could be eating, washing dishes, or simply walking with awareness by bringing your attention to sensations and details. Nature walks help you in paying attention to all your senses, thus giving you a chance to fully engage with the present moment. In the hours of quiet contemplation when you focus on your breath and senses, and let your thoughts pass without any kind of attachment, you allow yourself to act in the non-action mode. Also, in this mode, you can pursue your love for creativity and allow yourself to express yourself through the medium of creative and expressive arts. Try to align your actions and the state of being with the Wu Wei principles to witness the most surprising result of flowing in harmony with nature.

If you can spend some days being in the Wu Wei mode, that is living without stressing your mind, rather embracing the stillness, when this Wu Wei mode is over, you will feel rejuvenated because you will recognize what is your unique strength and how you do things in your natural, authentic way. You will get back your energy and as a result, you can work with a refreshing perspective.

Without exerting any force, in the Wu Wei state, you attain an inner harmony where your natural, free-flowing state of being is aligned with the spontaneous creative manifestation.

Acting in harmony with your natural being by following the Wu Wei way means you are allowing your uniqueness and naturalness to enter your home without any obstruction that would have acted as an external force to stop you from being one with yourself. Therefore, for me, Wu Wei is a nice way to spend some time with my inner self. Sometimes, it acts like a tool for self-discovery, and other times, it acts like a reminder of my potential when I do things with my most authentic self.

Sometimes, you get into the state of doing or being, but after some time, you see that all those stressful hours have unnecessarily burdened your mind. This may result from a lack of clarity, and during these hours, you spend time overthinking. However, instead of thinking aimlessly, if you can spend time in Wu Wei mode, you discover that these moments with effortless action offer you calm and clarity. Moreover, you will feel refreshed when you return to your active mode after spending some Wu Wei hours living in your natural order. When you are back, you can feel how essential this peace was for your well-being.

This is how Wu Wei can bring your mind to the most peaceful state by simply doing nothing. Because when you focus on your mental, emotional, and spiritual well-being by practicing the art of Wu Wei, you will allow your mind, body, and soul to feel calm and content.

And within that stillness, you will hear the echoes from within. Have you ever witnessed the miracles of living in harmony with your natural flow?

# Cherishing the Joy of Little Things with Hygge

It's all about finding joy,
In the little things that you often ignored.
It's all about learning the secrets of celebrating life
From the beauty the ordinary moments behold.

The Danish concept of Hygge (pronounced *hoo-gah*) is a blissful art that encompasses a feeling of coziness. And within this coziness, you find contentment which is essential for your well-being. The main purpose of this Hygge lifestyle is to celebrate every little thing in your life so that you can find happiness within. Hygge is the quality of coziness that brings you contentment and becomes a purpose of your well-being.

Therefore, the true essence of Hygge lies in cherishing the beauty of your everyday things, and thus, it is the pursuit of happiness that you will find only in the little things of life. If you can find the little things that make you happy from within, it helps you to find the inner calm too.

To practice Hygge, you need to create your own Hygge nook which is the corner of your house where you can nurture a sense of calm, comfort, and contentment. This is all about creating a special spot in your home where you can relax and unwind. For this purpose, you need to create a space where the only illumination will be soft lighting with candles and a cozy environment with a soft blanket. You can also decorate the space with comfortable furniture to add another level of coziness to the place. In addition, you can bring fresh flowers and indoor plants to give the space a refreshing look. Spend this quality time with your dear ones and share conversations and laughter to celebrate the little things together.

Remember to be attentive and fully present in the moments of happiness by bringing all your focus to cherish the Hygge hours. For relaxation, you can read a book or listen to your favorite music. However, prefer to listen to calming music during this time because it's all about finding calm in the brace of coziness. You can also cook a special dish to celebrate your Hygge hours with your loved ones. Wear soft and comfortable clothes, and practice self-care by engaging in different activities to nourish your mind, body, and soul. You can also spend some time journaling your thoughts.

Another way of practicing Hygge is having a walk in nature and enjoying this small retreat that you are gifting to yourself to improve your overall well-being. Make sure that you disconnect from technology and take a break from all types of digital screens during Hygge hours to cherish peaceful and happy moments with your dear ones.

When you are stressed, finding a solution is the only way to bring you the much-awaited relief. But when you are unable to find the solution right at this moment, it is necessary to think of it with a calm mind. In such moments, cherishing the joy of little things by embracing the coziness can give you relief from stress, and within that calmness, you will have better clarity about your vision. Enjoying the simple pleasures in life, and celebrating everyday happiness in little things – doesn't it sound peaceful to everyone?

I am sure you will certainly find something to cherish right at this moment. Maybe something very ordinary, yet, something very beautiful.

Let's cherish happiness in the Hygge way!

# CHAPTER TWENTY-SIX

# Celebrating Everyday Happiness with Lykke

The everyday moments bring me
A message of mundaneness
Where I find my solace
Tuning into my inner harmony.

When it comes to finding happiness in everyday things, there is a beautiful art called Lykke. It is the Danish way to celebrate your everyday life, balance your work and personal life, and stay calm from within.

Whenever I get stuck amidst multitasking, I make a priority list, and executing the tasks accordingly helps in doing them with ease. The same happens for our life's essential things. When you find peace while doing all the jobs in the right manner, there comes the art of finding happiness, which I am talking about. It is Lykke (pronounced *lick-uh*), a Scandinavian concept that means happiness.

Isn't it a beautiful reminder to us that Happiness is as simple as saying Lykke!

If you want to celebrate life and find calm and contentment in the everyday moments, you should follow Lykke which teaches us how the six essential factors can make you happy every day. These factors are togetherness, freedom, health, money, trust, and kindness.

Let's have a look at the role of these six essential factors in the pursuit of happiness. You can practice Lykke by incorporating them into your daily life.

**Togetherness**: Who can deny the fact that being closer to your near and dear ones gives you immense pleasure and joy? And thus, this is a great way to celebrate your life. Wherever you may live in the world, when you come home and hug your dear ones with a broad smile, you are happy because your loved ones are happy. This is the key to finding happiness; more precisely, to celebrate happiness. There is no better way to celebrate your life's happiest hours together with your dear ones.

**Freedom**: Freedom is an essential factor in celebrating happiness. Being free from your everyday stress is indeed a blissful way. So, escape from the hectic life routine for one day and go far from this urban lifestyle. Celebrate your happiness in some lonely corner, being lost in the lap of nature. It's all about sharing your load with your dear ones so you can celebrate your freedom. It's also about honoring freedom so it can offer you a sense of happiness by decluttering unnecessary stress.

**Health and Money**: Health should be always the first priority in life. Many factors contribute to our well-being. Money is indeed a factor that can help you to achieve almost everything you want in life. However, money can't provide you with all the things to make you happy. Therefore, making a wise choice can pave the way toward happiness, balancing between health and money.

You can take small steps and grow healthy habits to focus on your well-being. You can practice habits like resting your body and mind whenever necessary, walking, meditating, healthy eating, spending time in nature, and some more good habits to nurture a healthy lifestyle.

**Trust**: Trust is another key factor that contributes to the pursuit of happiness by offering you a trustworthy environment that leads to a greater level of calm and contentment. It helps in achieving happiness by fostering a strong connection to society where we feel motivated, comfortable, and safe within our very own community.

Eventually, it helps us reduce anxiety by cherishing a more meaningful connection with people, which in turn, helps us embrace a sense of belongingness and acceptance.

**Kindness:** Being kind is one of the greatest ways you can celebrate your inner happiness. Kindness can fill your heart with happiness that will reflect the purity of your soul. When you show kindness to others, to everyone on this earth, slowly you will cultivate compassion for yourself too, and being compassionate to yourself is the key to celebrating happiness.

Well, as of now, I am going to choose Togetherness, Freedom, and Kindness, because I am planning to read a book with my sister, walk alone in nature, and do some self-care activities. This way, I am going to celebrate my happiness like a free bird singing its song!

What are you planning to celebrate happiness in the Lykke way?

# Giving Importance to Every Moment with Ichigo Ichie

This moment,
this very moment,
echoes to you
what is written in silence -
The message of eternal bliss.

I have been practicing Mindfulness for the last few years. In these years, I have learned how being mindful can be extremely helpful in every aspect of life. Practicing Mindfulness has always been a wonderful experience for me.

While researching for this book, when I came across the concept of Ichigo Ichie, I was happy to read what it means. Ichigo Ichie (pronounced *ee-chee-go ee-chee-eh*) is an art that comes from an age-old concept. This Japanese idiom encompasses the idea of 'being attentive to every moment.' Essentially, Ichigo Ichie means 'one time, one meeting', which could be roughly translated as 'once in a lifetime.' This mindful art acts as a reminder of impermanence and transience.

When I practice Ichigo Ichie as an art of finding calm and contentment, I use all my senses to build a deeper connection to my inner self by being present in the moment. And within that process, I discover the truths that hold the key to eternal bliss. Thus, for me, Ichigo Ichie paves the path toward inner harmony.

~

Celebrating every moment as special is a blissful thought. When you delve deeper, Ichigo Ichie will unfold to you the truth that is hidden in this present moment. Every moment comes in your life only once; therefore, you should enjoy every moment as once in a lifetime, or else it will slip away from your grip and will be lost forever.

When I came across the message of this art, I paused for one moment. When I realized the essence of Ichigo Ichie, it felt very peaceful. For a moment, I paused and looked around - my dad was reading the newspaper, my mom was cooking in the kitchen, my sister was having her evening snacks, and I was working on my laptop. When I uttered the message of Ichigo Ichie: every moment comes only once in a lifetime, I felt peace all around, as I found a serene bliss in my mind.

Summer was approaching here. The weather was pleasant, I felt the air very calm, and my heart was filled with peace and happiness.

It reminded me of the message once again - this moment, this very moment, whatever is in this moment, no matter how it may feel, this is yours. All you have is here and now – and this is the real essence of the art of practicing mindfulness with Ichigo Ichie.

> *"If you dive deeper, Ichigo Ichie will unlock the door*
> *towards your inner peace and it will whisper to your ears,*
> *that all you have is this present moment."*

Ichigo Ichie offers you a chance to appreciate the unique nature of every moment and each experience. Savoring the moment by engaging all your senses and bringing your attention to embrace the truth of transience, this art teaches you to value the impermanence and transient nature of time. Thus, it helps in learning the practice of treating every encounter as a special occurrence and honoring the meeting like a once-in-a-lifetime phenomenon.

This is why, when you are following this art, you need to focus on every minute detail happening in the present moment. While eating, pay attention to the senses involved in mindful eating – observe the taste, the smell, the texture, and every detail of the food on your plate. While talking to someone, practice active listening and be fully present in the conversation. Even when you are not eating but doing something else, engage all your senses and take note of the details. Nurture every connection to a deeper level with empathy and kindness. Value every moment because this art is a reminder of the truth that every moment is temporary, and thus, every moment is precious as it comes to you only once.

*"This moment will only come once in a lifetime, hold it in your grip so that it never be lost in the path to eternity."*

Before it slips away, meet yourself, your unique self of this present moment - have a meeting for a lifetime to yourself that belongs to this present moment, because the next moment is waiting for something new in its store, and the way you find yourself in this present moment, it is going to be different in the next moment. You have been in the process of becoming, by taking a new form in every other moment. So, why not give attention to your being in this present moment?

This moment is yours, live it to the fullest.

Meanwhile, try to hear what this moment brings to you. Does it echo something to you?

# CHAPTER TWENTY-EIGHT

# Realizing the Zeal of Life with Kefi

The birdsong in the morning,
The blooming tree dwindling in the breeze,
The buzz of the honey bees,
All of them remind me
of the beauty in simple living
and how to be happy from within.

It's been three years since I started working on this book and I am enjoying the process of authoring my third book. It is dusk here and I am enjoying this golden hour. The sky is covered with sparkling crimson, the neighborhood kids are playing in the road, and the flock of birds are returning home. I am watching them from my window and typing on my laptop about my experience.

I am enjoying writing in this way, relieving my day's stress and finding some moments for my love of writing and watching nature. The breeze is calming my mind and I am enjoying this.

I am enjoying all these little things and thus, I find peace of mind.

This is what I have learned about Kefi - the art that tells us how important is to cherish the joy of little things around you.

The word Kefi (pronounced *keh-fee*) means to celebrate the spirit of joy, passion, and enthusiasm by nurturing a sense of euphoria. This is the feeling when you overpower your emotions and let go of everything that comes as an obstacle in your way of embracing inner joy and contentment. Kefi is a reminder that this moment is all about being happy and celebrating happiness in your way - you feel happy, you feel content, you are aware of this present moment, and this means you are feeling Kefi!

Amidst the stress and anxiety of life's big things, often we forget to be mindful of the tiny things that bring us joy and happiness. This is why if we celebrate happiness in the Kefi way, it will be easier to find joy in little things which is extremely important to find calm and contentment.

I started working on this book to write about the ways of calm and contentment I learned. When I started researching different wellness concepts and philosophies from across the globe, at first, I thought it was my pursuit of happiness. But the more I researched, the more I realized that happiness is not something that you can define with a word. Happiness is not only a word; rather, it's a process, a journey, a quest.

Happiness is an inward journey and an eternal process. In this process, many truths will be revealed to you. This is what happened to me while writing this book. I had one such realization when I learned about Kefi, the art of happiness that teaches us how to feel the zeal of life.

Kefi is something beyond celebrating momentary happiness. **It is beyond everything that you define as the factors of happiness because it is something that you can only feel when you allow the feeling of happiness to be embraced in its entirety.**

Whether it is watching the flying birds, the blue sky over your head, enjoying the sunbeams touching your face, sipping your afternoon coffee, watching it rain and hearing the sounds of raindrops, feeling the calmness around and inhaling the smell of rain-bathed earth, every little thing can give you happiness. And Kefi is all about feeling every pulse of the happiness that can be found in little things in life.

I practice the art of Kefi with all the concepts I discussed in this book. Listening to the first bird songs in the hours of dawn, walking at my own pace with a calm and content heart, practicing contemplative meditation through arranging flowers, letting go of the past and everything that burdens me with pain and weighs me down, healing myself with the blissful reminders of acceptance, embracing my imperfections, glorifying my wounds and scars like they are my shining crown, showing gratitude through the art of appreciation, holding the lamp of compassion for others as well as practicing self-compassion, nurturing a delicate and affectionate bond with my inner child, nurturing a sense of purpose in everything I do, putting a part of me in my every work, engaging myself in a gradual process of self-improvement, setting boundaries to protect my peaceful living, enjoying my work, taking breaks in between my work schedule, embracing the warmth and coziness and taking a plunge into the relieving vibes, surrendering myself to the natural flow and trusting the universe, allowing myself to feel the sweetness of doing nothing, enjoying life with fun and fulfilment, spending time with nature, nurturing a deep connection with environment, watching the moon and finding peace in the whispers of night, nurturing work-life balance, celebrating everyday moments, practicing present moment awareness, and finally, cherishing the little things to live, laugh, and love by making every moment larger than life.

However, I would like to request you to practice Kefi in your own way because happiness is different for everyone and the definition and celebration of happiness differs for every individual. I want you to find your own unique way to practice Kefi and feel every pulse of happiness within your homebody.

I have experienced that Kefi is not only being happy but also allowing yourself to feel this joyful moment and let this pulse of happiness go deep down your body and soul; it is all about living in the present moment, by enjoying what is happening around you and allowing the feeling of joy to cherish the zeal of feeling alive – celebrating every pulse of your aliveness and counting your blessings. It's not only about feeling happy to the fullest but also feeling every pulse of happiness.

You can practice Kefi by showing gratitude for everything you have right now. You can also practice Kefi by connecting with your loved ones and being with them for a little longer. It's about dancing madly to your favorite song and watching the rainbow beyond the horizon.

You can also put into practice all the concepts and philosophies shared in this book.

Kefi cherishes every moment of happiness by making it an inevitable part of your being, and you will realize the true essence of Kefi only when you do it yourself. Only reading about Kefi is not enough, it is more about feeling than knowing from someone else.

*"Happiness is a choice. Happiness is a reminder that life is too short to fight with yourself, to ruin your joy for something that doesn't serve any purpose in your life. Happiness is like the morning song of birds, just sing it!"*

The route towards happiness differs for each person, and this is why the definition of happiness is different for you and me.

Happiness is eternal, happiness is your very own.

When you attain the Kefi state, only then you will realize the happiness in being true to yourself.

What a zeal to feel Kefi, isn't it?

# A Livsnjutare Sings!



*"Life isn't meant to be lived perfectly...but merely to be lived. Boldly, wildly, beautifully, uncertainly, imperfectly, magically lived.*
*- Mandy Hale"*

When it comes to finding happiness in little things, we often find it hard, as we have been living life for a long time with all the things that make our lives happier, more comfortable, and more successful. But when it comes to making your life more meaningful and purposeful, you return to your roots.

The root that has been your very own abode of happiness. The root where you were happy with your small circle of friends, an adequate amount of entertainment, and the little things like a warm hug from your sibling, a bar of chocolate from your father, and the meal with your favorite dish, cooked by your mother.

There was a time when we were happy with all these things. Only these things. There was a dream, there was ambition, and there was a routine to follow because we wanted to have all the desired things in our arms, someday, in the future. But the main purpose of our living was to be happy with whatever we had at that moment. Whatever we had with us, we were happy with them all.

Life was easy and simple because we had the purpose of being Livsnjutare with us.

The word Livsnjutare (pronounced *leev-snoo-tah-reh*) means being happy with your life and living your life to the fullest. The person who loves life deeply and wants to live it to the extreme is called Livsnjutare. When I fell into the trap of despair, it was hard to find a way to get rid of the trap. All along I was searching for a tiny ray of life - the ray called Hope.

After the phase was over when I was contemplating my journey of despair, I discovered that it was all about finding Hope through the tiny things in life, and unbeknownst to me, they kept me alive all through the darkness. They were my hope for living my life to the fullest, and this is why I believe in the concept of Livsnjutare. The one who has returned to the mainstream of life after living on the other side of life, knows it best that it is all about the little things that gift you hope, love, and peace. This is how you learn to find the ray of hope, fall in love with your life, and find peace in the mundane things.

Being a Livsnjutare is all about your journey to the root. It is all about finding happiness in your life. It is all about embracing your life and live, love, laugh to its extreme. As I discovered this blissful truth of life, I planned to make a beautiful collage with them, and gradually, the collage took the shape of this book!

# Bibliography

1. Longhurst, E. N. (2018). *Japonisme: Ikigai, Forest Bathing, Wabi-sabi and more* (Kindle Edition). Publisher: Harper Thorsons.
2. Haas, S. (2020). *Why Be Happy? The Japanese Way of Acceptance* (Kindle Edition). Publisher: John Murray One.
3. Kempton, B. (2018). *Wabi Sabi: Japanese Wisdom for a Perfectly Imperfect Life* (Kindle Edition). Publisher: Piatkus.
4. Navarro, T. (2018). *Kintsugi: Embrace your imperfections and find happiness - the Japanese way* (Kindle Edition). Publisher: Yellow Kite.
5. Nylund, J. (2018). *Sisu: The Finnish Art of Courage* (Kindle Edition). Publisher: Gaia.
6. Pantzar, K. (2022). *Everyday Sisu: Tapping into Finnish Fortitude for a Happier, More Resilient Life* (Kindle Edition). Publisher: TarcherPerigee.
7. Pantzar, K. (2018). *Finding Sisu: THE FINNISH WAY* (Kindle Edition). Publisher: Hodder & Stoughton.
8. García, H. & Miralles, F. (2017). *Ikigai: Japanese secret to a long and happy life* (Kindle Edition). Publisher: Cornerstone Digital.
9. Harvey, S. (2019). Kaizen: *The Japanese Method for Transforming Habits, One Small Step at a Time* (Kindle Edition) Publisher: Bluebird.
10. Maurer, R. (2014). *One Small Step Can Change Your Life: The Kaizen Way* (Kindle Edition) Publisher: Workman Publishing Company.
11. Hong, E. (2019). The Power of Nunchi: *The Korean Secret to Happiness and Success* (Kindle Edition) Publisher: Cornerstone Digital.
12. Lynda, B. (2018). *The Little Book of Fika: The Uplifting Daily Ritual of the Swedish Coffee Break* (Kindle Edition). Publisher: Andrews McMeel Publishing, LLC.
13. Mecking, O. (2020). *Niksen: Embracing the Dutch Art of Doing*

*Nothing* (Kindle Edition). Publisher: Piatkus.

14. D'Souza, S. (2021). *Susegad: The Goan Art of Contentment* (Kindle Edition). Publisher: Ebury Press.
15. Mona, C. (2022). *Kaizen, Shinrin-yoku, Kintsugi: The triple Japanese way to find happiness and life purpose* (Kindle Edition)
16. Dunne, L. (2017) *Lagom: The Swedish Art of Balanced Living* (Kindle edition). Publisher: Gaia.
17. Miralles, F. & García H. (2020). *The Book of Ichigo Ichie* (Kindle Edition). Publisher: Quercus.
18. Wiking, M. (2016). *The Little Book of Hygge: The million copy bestselling guide to the Danish art of living well - the perfect mindfulness gift* (Penguin Life) Kindle Edition. Publisher: Penguin.
19. Wiking, M. (2019). *Little Book of Lykke* (Kindle Edition). Publisher: Penguin.
20. Hayden, B. (2019). *Hygge: Unlock the Danish Art of Coziness and Happiness* (Scandinavian Life Philosophies) Kindle Edition.
21. Hayden, B. (2019). *Lagom: What You Need to Know About the Swedish Art of Living a Balanced Life (Scandinavian Life Philosophies)* Kindle Edition.
22. White, A. & James, R. (2017) *Hygge: Introduction to The Danish Art of Cozy Living* (Kindle Edition).
23. Aiden, N. (2021) *Bathing in the Forest: A Healing Guide to Self-Love, Reducing Stress, and Changing Your Life by Connecting with Nature* (Kindle Edition).
24. Lomas, T. (2018) *Translating Happiness: A Cross-Cultural Lexicon of Well-Being* (Kindle Edition). Publisher: The MIT Press.

BIBLIOGRAPHY

<h1 style="text-align:center">References</h1>


**Arbejdsglæde**

1. Team The Curiosity Approach, "Curious about what "Arbejdsglæde" means?", *The Curiosity Approach,* https://www.thecuriosityapproach.com/blog/curious-about-what-arbejdsglaede-means

2. Marla Gottschalk, "Joy at Work: How about a little "Arbejdsglæde"?", *Marla Gottschalk Blog,* July 4, 2013, https://marlagottschalk.com/2013/07/04/joy-at-work-how-about-a-little-arbejdsglaede/

3. Michael Metcalf, "Arbejdsglæde: the Danish concept of happiness at work", *Timetastic,* https://timetastic.co.uk/blog/arbejdsglaede-the-danish-concept-of-happiness-at-work/

4. Nicola Robey, "The Danish art of enjoying work", *Stranger Collective,* https://stranger-collective.com/the-danish-art-of-enjoying-work/

5. Justin Timmer, The Scandinavian secret to workplace happiness, *Measuremen,* https://measuremen.io/blog/workplace-happiness/

~

**Fika**

1. Agneta Yngve a b, Henrik Scander c, Stina Almroth d, "Taking a closer look at the Swedish coffee break, "fika"", *International Journal of Gastronomy and Food Science,* Volume 33, September 2023, 100775, https://www.sciencedirect.com/science/article/pii/S1878450X23001178

2. Leah Harper, "Fika, four-week holidays – and zero overtime: Sweden's stunningly healthy work culture", *The Guardian,* 8 Nov 2023, https://www.theguardian.com/lifeandstyle/2023/nov/08/fika-four-week-holidays-and-zero-overtime-swedens-stunningly-healthy-work-culture

3. The Science of Happiness Podcast, "Feeling Overworked? Take a Fika Break (The Science of Happiness Podcast)", *Greater Good*, May 25, 2023, *Magazine*, https://greatergood.berkeley.edu/podcasts/item/feeling_overworked_take_a_fika_break

4. Francesca Murdaca, "Fika: The Swedish switch-off method that's *almost* too good to be true (and yes, it involves coffee and cake)", *Glamour*, 18 November 2022, https://www.glamourmagazine.co.uk/article/what-is-fika-swedish-wellbeing

5. Video by Björn Nilsson (Executive producer: Camelia Sadeghzadeh), "The Swedish tradition that can make you happier at work", *BBC*, 9 November 2023, https://www.bbc.com/reel/video/p0bmzygz/the-swedish-tradition-that-can-make-you-happier-at-work

~

### Friluftsliv

1. Maddy Savage, "Friluftsliv: The Nordic concept of getting outdoors", *BBC*, 11 December 2017, https://www.bbc.com/worklife/article/20171211-friluftsliv-the-nordic-concept-of-getting-outdoors

2. Lauren Geall, "Friluftsliv: why embracing the Nordic concept could help to boost your mental health this winter", *Stylist*, 2022, https://www.stylist.co.uk/health/mental-health/what-is-friluftsliv-open-air-living-nature-mental-health-benefits/445876

3. Sandi Schwartz, "How Friluftsliv Can Help You Live an Open-Air Life to Boost Well-Being", *Success*, July 31, 2024, https://www.success.com/friluftsliv-open-air-life/

4. Rachel Dixon, "The Norwegian secret: how friluftsliv boosts health and happiness", *The Guardian*, Wed 27 Sep 2023, https://www.theguardian.com/lifeandstyle/2023/sep/27/the-norwegian-secret-how-friluftsliv-boosts-health-and-happiness

5. Sasha Brady, "Embrace winter like a Norwegian this year by practising 'friluftsliv'", *Lonely Planet,* Oct 1, 2020, https://www.lonelyplanet.com/news/what-is-friluftsliv

6. Sweta Akundi, "The 'friluftsliv' way of embracing the outdoors like the Norwegians", *The Hindu*, January 12, 2021, https://www.thehindu.com/life-and-style/friluftsliv-norwegian-lifestyle-of-embracing-outdoors/article33550184.ece

7. Fiona McKinna, "Friluftsliv, Your Life Outdoors", *Living a Nordic Life*, Feb 16, 2021, https://www.livinganordiclife.com/post/friluftsliv-life-outdoors

8. Team Visit Norway, "FRILUFTSLIV: the Norwegian love for the outdoors", *Visit Norway*, https://www.visitnorway.com/things-to-do/outdoor-activities/friluftsliv/

9. Kari Leibowitz, PhD, "How Scandinavians Do It: An Open Air Life", *National Nordic Museum*, November 27, 2023, https://nordicmuseum.org/news/leibowitz-open-air-life

~

**Gökotta**

1. Claire Munnings, "How to feel more awake in the morning: try the mindful Swedish practice of gökotta for better energy and productivity," *Stylist*, 2023, https://www.stylist.co.uk/fitness-health/wellbeing/how-to-feel-more-awake-gokotta/786434

2. Jonny Thomson, "Gökotta: How to experience nature the Swedish way", *Big Think*, April 14, 2023, https://bigthink.com/neuropsych/gokotta-swedish-experience-nature/

3. Meg Warren-Lister, "Gökotta is the latest Scandinavian wellness trend to try this summer", *Women's Health*, 22 June 2023, https://www.womenshealthmag.com/uk/health/a44267343/gokotta-scandinavian-wellness-summer/

4. Swiish Team, "Gökotta: The Trend to Try", *Swiish*, https://blog.swiish.com/gokotta-the-trend-to-try/

5. Adithyan P, "Rise and Shine With Gökotta, the Swedish Ritual That'll Make You a Morning Person", *News 18*, May 31, 2023, https://www.news18.com/viral/rise-and-shine-with-gokotta-the-swedish-ritual-thatll-make-you-a-morning-person-7960861.html

6. Jassila Sikkandar, "Gokotta: Embracing the Swedish Philosophy of Morning Serenity", *Medium,* https://medium.com/@sanaedtech/gokotta-embracing-the-swedish-philosophy-of-morning-serenity-f80525a99ccc

7. Nesi Zelenkova, "The Swedish concept of gökotta – listen to the morning birdsong", *203 Travel Challenges,* https://www.203challenges.com/the-swedish-concept-of-gokotta-listen-to-the-morning-birdsong/

8. Jolanta Burke Ph.D. (Reviewed by Lybi Ma), "How Seeing and Listening to Birds Can Improve Well-Being", *Psychology Today*, January 5, 2023, https://www.psychologytoday.com/intl/blog/the-good-life-ritual/202301/how-seeing-and-listening-to-birds-can-improve-well-being

~

**Hygge**
1. *Wikipedia*, Hygge, https://en.wikipedia.org/wiki/Hygge

2. Stacey Colino (Medically Reviewed by Allison Young, MD), "What Is Hygge, and Why Is It Good for Your Well-Being?", *Everyday Health,* Updated on November 3, 2022, https://www.everydayhealth.com/wellness/what-is-hygge-and-why-is-it-good-for-your-wellbeing/

3. Jodi Clarke, MA, LPC/MHSP (Medically reviewed by Carly Snyder, MD), "Benefits of the Cozy Wellness Trend Hygge", *VeryWellMind*, October 07, 2021, https://www.verywellmind.com/health-benefits-of-hygge-4164281

4. Justin Parkinson, "Hygge: A heart-warming lesson from Denmark", *BBC News Magazine*, 2 October 2015, https://www.bbc.com/news/magazine-34345791

5. Team Calm (Clinically reviewed by Dr. Chris Mosunic, PhD, RD, MBA), "How to practice hygge and celebrate life's simple pleasures", *Calm*, https://www.calm.com/blog/how-to-practice-hygge

6. Lyndsey Matthews, "What Is Hygge? Everything You Need To Know About The Danish Lifestyle Trend", *Country Living,*

Updated: Dec 5, 2018, https://www.countryliving.com/life/a41187/what-is-hygge-things-to-know-about-the-danish-lifestyle-trend/

7. Team Curious Motion, "What Is Hygge, and How Can It Help Our Wellbeing?", *Curious Motion,* November 24, 2023, https://curiousmotion.org.uk/what-is-hygge-and-how-can-it-help-our-wellbeing/

8. Team, Visit Denmark, "What is hygge?", *Visit Denmark,* https://www.visitdenmark.com/denmark/things-do/danish-culture/what-hygge

9. Anne Roderique-Jones, "I Practiced Hygge and It's Kind of the Best Thing Ever", *Self,* December 25, 2018, https://www.self.com/story/practicing-hygge-danish-lifestyle

~

**Ichigo Ichie**

1. *Wikipedia,* Ichi-go ichi-e, https://en.wikipedia.org/wiki/Ichi-go_ichi-e

2. Héctor García & Francesc Miralles, "What Is Ichigo Ichie? 10 Rules Of The Japanese Way To Happiness", *MindBodyGreen,* December 30, 2019, https://www.mindbodygreen.com/articles/what-is-ichigo-ichie-10-rules-of-the-japanese-way-to-happiness

3. A. Broadway, "The Meaning of Ichigo Ichie: Making the Most of Every Moment", *Sen Bird Tea,* November 23, 2022, https://senbirdtea.com/blogs/japan-culture/the-meaning-of-ichigo-ichie-making-the-most-of-every-moment

4. Nishil Kothary, "Ichigo Ichie: The Meaning Behind the Powerful Japanese Phrase", *Earth's Corner,* April 11, 2019, https://www.earths-corner.com/ichi-go-ichi-e-a-japanese-phrase-the-world-should-live-by/

5. Rosetta Stone, "There's a Word for That: Embracing the Present with Ichi-go Ichi-e (いちごいちえ)", July 21, 2022, *Rosetta Stone Blog,* https://blog.rosettastone.com/words-beyond-translation-ichi-go-ichi-e/

~

**Ikebana**

1. Wikipedia, Ikebana, https://en.wikipedia.org/wiki/Ikebana

2. Mehwash Hussain, "Ikebana: The blooming harmony", *The Hindu*, August 18, 2024, https://www.thehindu.com/children/ikebana-the-blooming-harmony/article68495498.ece

3. Flower Aura, "The Art of Ikebana: Exploring Japanese Flower Arranging as a Meditative Practice", *Flower Aura*, https://www.floweraura.com/blog/the-art-of-ikebana-exploring-japanese-flower-arranging-meditative-practice

4. Kamila, "Blooming Wellness - The Healing Power of Ikebana", *Nature to Go,* https://www.naturetogo.ie/post/blooming-wellness-the-healing-power-of-ikebana

5. The Floral Society, "Everything You Need To Know About Ikebana Floral Design", *The Floral Society*, https://www.thefloralsociety.com/blogs/ikebana-arrangements/everything-you-need-to-know-about-ikebana-floral-design

6. Gwyneth, "How Ikebana Arrangements Help You Feel Calm", *Flowers by Gwyneth*, https://www.flowersbygwyneth.com.au/how-ikebana-can-help-you-feel-calm/

~

**Ikigai**

1. *Wikipedia*, Ikigai, https://en.wikipedia.org/wiki/Ikigai

2. Jeffrey Gaines, Ph.D. , "The Philosophy of Ikigai: 3 Examples About Finding Purpose", *Positive Psychology*, 17 Nov 2020, https://positivepsychology.com/ikigai/

3. Elizabeth Perry, ACC, "What is ikigai and how can it change my life?", *BetterUp*,
October 25, 2024, https://www.betterup.com/blog/what-is-ikigai

4. Team Calm (Clinically reviewed by Dr. Chris Mosunic, PhD, RD, MBA), "Ikigai: what it is and how to use ikigai to find your purpose", *Calm*, https://www.calm.com/blog/ikigai

5. Nell Derick Debevoise, "The Power Of Purpose: How Ikigai Can Help Us Live Longer", *Forbes*, Oct 6, 2023, https://www.forbes.com/sites/nelldebevoise/2023/10/06/the-power-of-purpose-how-ikigai-can-help-us-live-longer/

~

**Kaizen**

1. *Wikipedia*, Kaizen, https://en.wikipedia.org/wiki/Kaizen

2. Jonny Thomson, "To make great changes in your life, follow the philosophy of kaizen", *Big Think*, July 30, 2022, https://bigthink.com/smart-skills/kaizen/

3. Vivek Kumar, "What is the Kaizen technique? Exploring The Japanese Philosophy That Helps in Mental Well-Being", *OnlyMyHealth*, Jan 21, 2025, https://www.onlymyhealth.com/what-is-kaizen-technique-japanese-philosophy-that-helps-in-mental-well-being-12977824044

4. Elizabeth Perry, ACC, "Using the Kaizen method for personal growth and success", *BetterUp*, June 8, 2024, https://www.betterup.com/blog/kaizen

5. Minda Zetlin, "Kaizen, the Japanese Practice of Continuous Improvement, Can Help You Reach All Your Goals. Here's How", *Inc*, JUN 11, 2019, https://www.inc.com/minda-zetlin/kaizen-continuous-improvement-self-improvement-1-percent-goals-thomas-oppong.html

~

**Kansha**

1. Jeremy Sutton, Ph.D, "5 Benefits of Journaling for Mental Health", *Positive Psychology*, 14 May 2018, https://positivepsychology.com/benefits-of-journaling/

2. Sheldon Reid, "Journaling for Mental Health and Wellness", *HelpGuide.org*, July 19, 2024, https://www.helpguide.org/mental-health/wellbeing/journaling-for-mental-health-and-wellness

3. Kin North, "Kansha, Cultivating Sincere Gratitude", *Kin North Blog*, May 05, 2021, https://kinnorth.com/blogs/journal/kansha-cultivating-sincere-gratitude

4. Ranya Iyer, "Kansha: The Yin & Yang of Gratitude", Oct 9, 2024, *Kintsugi Art Studio*, https://www.kintsugiartstudio.com/post/kansha-the-yin-yang-of-gratitude

~

**Kefi**

1. Celinne Da Costa, Words Beyond Translation: Kefi, *Rosetta Stone*, November 30, 2017, https://blog.rosettastone.com/words-beyond-translation-kefi/

2. Alexis Arabia (blog post written by Theodora Maios), "ΚΕΦΙ: a Greek word that can't be translated", *NEOS COSMOS*, 21 September 2017, https://neoskosmos.com/en/2017/09/21/features/%CE%9Aefi-a-greek-word-that-cant-be-translated/

3. Lemon & Olives, "The Meaning Of Kefi | Finding Your Kefi", *Lemon & Olives*, 10 August 2023, https://www.lemonandolives.com/meaning-of-kefi/

4. Greek Boston, "What is the Meaning of Kefi for Greeks?", *Greek Boston*, https://www.greekboston.com/culture/modern-history/kefi/

~

**Kintsugi**

1. *Wikipedia*, Kintsugi, https://en.wikipedia.org/wiki/Kintsugi

2. Terushi Sho, "Kintsugi: Japan's ancient art of embracing imperfection", *BBC*, 9 January 2021, https://www.bbc.com/travel/article/20210107-kintsugi-japans-ancient-art-of-embracing-imperfection

3. Rosalind Jana, "The Japanese craft that helps us heal", *BBC*, 13 September 2022, https://www.bbc.com/culture/article/20220822-why-we-are-drawn-to-mending-things

4. Georgia Green, "What is kintsugi and why is it so good at slowing down your mind?", *Stylist*, 2025, https://www.stylist.co.uk/health/mental-health/what-is-kintsugi/954482

5. Tiffany Ayuda, "How the Japanese art of Kintsugi can help you deal with stressful situations", *NBC News*, April 26, 2018, https://www.nbcnews.com/better/health/how-japanese-art-technique-kintsugi-can-help-you-be-more-ncna866471

~

**Koselig**

1. Tim Lomas, "The importance of being koselig", *The Huffpost*, Mar 2, 2016, https://www.huffpost.com/entry/the-importance-of-being-k_b_9365554

2. Dawn Potter, PsyD, "How the Norwegian Concept of Koselig Can Get You Through the Winter", *Cleveland Clinic*, December 16, 2022, https://health.clevelandclinic.org/how-koselig-can-get-you-through-the-winter

3. Kayleigh Dray, "Dark evenings getting you down? Try the Nordic wellness trend of koselig", *Stylist*, 2022, https://www.stylist.co.uk/health/mental-health/koselig-nordic-wellbeing-trend/563689

4. Juliette Sivertsen, "The art of koselig: How to become more Norwegian for winter", *The Post*, July 25, 2023, https://www.thepost.co.nz/wellbeing/350041960/art-koselig-how-become-more-norwegian-winter

5. Jason Wilson, "What Is Koselig? How to Incorporate This Norwegian Concept Into Your Life", *Reader's Digest,* Jan. 12, 2023, https://www.rd.com/article/koselig/

6. Ingrid Opstad, "Koselig – The Norwegian Concept that will Help You Through Winter", *That Scandinavian Feeling*, https://www.thatscandinavianfeeling.com/lifestyle/norwegian-concept-koselig

7. Team CNN, "Where coziness meets happiness: Norway's koselig and Denmark's hygge", *CNN Health*, Wed May 1, 2019, https://edition.cnn.com/2019/05/01/health/gallery/norwegian-nature-hapiness-koselig-hygge-wisdom-project/index.html

8. David G. Allan, "Why are Norwegians so happy? In a word: 'koselig'", *CNN Health*, Mon July 1, 2019, https://edition.cnn.com/2019/04/30/health/norway-koselig-hygge-cozy-nature-chasing-life-wisdom-project/index.html

~

**Lagom**

1. *Wikipedia*, Lagom, https://en.wikipedia.org/wiki/Lagom

2. Lola Akinmade Åkerström, "The Swedish word that's displacing hygge", *BBC,* 24 August 2017, https://www.bbc.com/

travel/article/20170818-the-swedish-word-thats-displacing-hygge

3. Lola Akinmade Åkerström, "Lagom: Is this the secret to Swedish happiness?", *Adventure*, March 22, 2018, https://adventure.com/lagom-swedish-secret-of-living-well/

4. Leah Sinclair, "Why the Nordic concepts of 'kos' and 'lagom' could be the key to getting through winter", *Stylist,* 2023, https://www.stylist.co.uk/home/kos-lagom-nordic-wellbeing-trends/746469

5. Jonny Thomson, "The Swedish philosophy of lagom: how "just enough" is all you need", *Big Think*, Published in August 2022, Updated in August 2023, https://bigthink.com/thinking/swedish-philosophy-lagom-just-enough/

6. Ayesha Singh, "Living the lagom life: Swedish philosophy that focuses on being content", *The New Indian Express,* 10 Sep 2022, https://www.newindianexpress.com/lifestyle/health/2022/Sep/10/living-the-lagom-life-swedish-philosophy-that-focuses-on-being-content-2496254.html

7. Starre Julia Vartan, "Embrace the Swedish "Lagom" Lifestyle to Reduce Stress and Live More Moderately", *LifeHacker*, October 25, 2017, https://lifehacker.com/embrace-the-swedish-lagom-lifestyle-to-reduce-stress-1819730614

~

**Lykke**

1. Megy Karydes, "Move Over Hygge, 6 Ways To Live More Lykke", *Forbes*, Jan 29, 2018, https://www.forbes.com/sites/megykarydes/2018/01/29/move-over-hygge-6-ways-to-live-more-lykke/

2. Megy Karydes, "How to Lykke Like You Mean It", *Forbes*, Jan 29, 2018, https://www.forbes.com/sites/megykarydes/2018/01/29/how-to-lykke-like-you-mean-it/

3. John Crace, "The Little Book of Lykke: The Danish Search for the World's Happiest People by Meik Wiking – digested read", *The Guardian*, 10 Sep 2017, https://www.theguardian.com/books/2017/sep/10/the-little-book-of-lykke-meik-wiking-danish-happiest-people-digested-read

4. Boudicca Fox-Leonard, "A Lykke life: the six pillars of happiness that keep the whole world smiling", *The Telegraph*, 10 September 2017, https://www.telegraph.co.uk/health-fitness/mind/lykke-life-six-pillars-pf-happiness-found-across-globe/

5. Team The Everygirl, "Lykke Is the New Hygge and It's All We've Ever Needed", *The Everygirl*, February 21, 2019, https://theeverygirl.com/what-is-lykke/

~

## Mångata

1. *Wikitionary*, mångata, https://en.wiktionary.org/wiki/m%C3%A5ngata

2. Victoria Restrepo, "Do you know what the word "mangata" means?", *Victoria Restrepo Blog*, April 22, 2024, https://vrestrepo.com/do-you-know-what-the-word-mangata-means/

3. Kristin, "Mångata: Have you ever watched a moonbeam?", *Untranslatable*, Dec 08, 2023, https://untranslatable.substack.com/p/mangata-have-you-ever-watched-a-moonbeam

~

## Meraki

1. Cary Yoga, "The Significance Of Meraki", *Cary Yoga Collective*, Sep 29, 2022, https://caryyogacollective.com/the-significance-of-meraki/

2. Kirsty, "Meaning Of Meraki", *Travel with Meraki*, https://travelwithmeraki.com/meaning-of-meraki/

3. Erik Brown, "Meraki: An Ancient Greek Secret For A Rich Life", *X (Published in Mind Cafe)*, Jan 27, 2022, https://medium.com/mind-cafe/meraki-an-ancient-greek-secret-for-a-rich-life-bdccc23c948a

~

## Niksen

1. *Wikipedia*, Niksen, https://en.wikipedia.org/wiki/Niksen

2. Olga Mecking, "The Dutch solution to busyness that captivated the world", *BBC*, 23 May 2023, https://www.bbc.com/travel/article/20230522-the-dutch-solution-to-busyness-that-

captivated-the-world

3. Sophia Gottfried, "Niksen Is the Dutch Lifestyle Concept of Doing Nothing—And You're About to See It Everywhere", *TIME*, July 12, 2019, https://time.com/5622094/what-is-niksen/

4. Viv Groskop, "The art of doing nothing: have the Dutch found the answer to burnout culture?", *The Guardian*, Wed 7 Feb 2024, https://www.theguardian.com/lifeandstyle/2024/feb/07/the-art-of-doing-nothing-have-the-dutch-found-the-answer-to-burnout-culture

5. Stuart Heritage, "People just do nothing: is the Dutch concept of niksen the best way to relax?", *The Guardian*, Mon 22 Jul 2019, https://www.theguardian.com/lifeandstyle/shortcuts/2019/jul/22/people-just-do-nothing-is-the-dutch-concept-of-niksen-the-best-way-to-relax

6. Najib Shah, "Come, let us niksen", *The Economic Times*, Feb 15, 2024, https://economictimes.indiatimes.com/opinion/speaking-tree/come-let-us-niksen/articleshow/107731925.cms?from=mdr

7. TOI Lifestyle Desk, "Niksen: The Dutch philosophy of the art of doing nothing", *Times of India (Times Entertainment)*, Apr 7, 2024, https://timesofindia.indiatimes.com/life-style/soul-search/niksen-the-dutch-philosophy-of-the-art-of-doing-nothing/photostory/109104241.cms

8. Kevin Dickinson, "Ease productivity overload with "niksen," the Dutch art of doing nothing", *Big Think*, February 13, 2023, https://bigthink.com/the-learning-curve/niksen/

9. Susan Devaney, "What is Niksen? The Dutch lifestyle concept that allows us to do nothing", *Vogue India*, 21 July 2019, https://www.vogue.co.uk/article/what-is-niksen-do-nothing-trend-dutch

~

## Nunchi

1. *Wikipedia*, Nunchi, https://en.wikipedia.org/wiki/Nunchi

2. Euny Hong, "What Is Nunchi? 8 Rules For This Korean Secret To Emotional Intelligence", *MindBodyGreen*, November 29, 2019,

https://www.mindbodygreen.com/articles/what-is-nunchi

3. Melissa Kim, "How to use nunchi, a Korean 'superpower,' to achieve your New Year's resolutions", *NBC News*, Jan. 7, 2020, https://www.nbcnews.com/news/asian-america/how-use-nunchi-korean-superpower-achieve-your-new-year-s-n1111326

4. Adrienne Matei, "What is 'nunchi', the Korean secret to happiness?", *The Guardian*, Mon 11 Nov 2019, https://www.theguardian.com/lifeandstyle/2019/nov/11/what-is-nunchi-the-korean-secret-to-happiness

~

**Omoiyari**

1. The Ikigai Podcast, "037 – Exploring the Japanese concept of Omoiyari", *Ikigai Tribe*, February 28, 2022, https://ikigaitribe.com/podcasts/podcast37/

2. Arzaqia Luthfi Yani, "Omoiyari: The Reason Why Japanese are Empathetic and Considerate", *Tokhimo*, May 14, 2022, https://www.tokhimo.com/post/omoiyari-the-reason-why-japanese-are-empathetic-and-considerate-1

3. Ruediger Oehlmann, Haajarah Chaudhry, "Omoiyari and Reference Place: Team Support based on Multi-modal Communication", *Procedia Computer Science, Volume 22, 2013, Pages 1126-1135, https://www.sciencedirect.com/science/article/pii/S1877050913009927*

~

**Oubaitori**

1. Kayleigh Dray, "Comparison culture: as we head out of lockdown, we need to embrace the Japanese concept of "oubaitori"", *Stylist*, https://www.stylist.co.uk/health/mental-health/oubaitori-comparison-culture-wellbeing/488138

2. Narayani Ganesh, "Japanese Concepts that Inform and Inspire", *Times of India*, Mar 9, 2024, https://timesofindia.indiatimes.com/speaking-tree/daily-ecstasy/japanese-concepts-that-inform-and-inspire/articleshow/108354873.cms

3. Yamato Magazine, "5 Powerful Japanese Concepts For Creating A Positive Mental Health Routine", *Yamato Magazine*, 19th Dec 2019, https://yamatomagazine.home.blog/2019/12/19/5-powerful-japanese-concepts-for-creating-a-positive-mental-health-routine/

4. Jake Hallows, "The Japanese Concept of 'Oubaitori'", *TravelwithLanguages.com*, https://travelwithlanguages.com/blog/japanese-oubaitori.html

5. Smitha Murthy, "Moments with Smitha Murthy || Lessons from flowers: The Japanese concept of oubaitori", *MyndStories*, 20 September 2022, https://myndstories.com/allpodcast/moments-with-smitha-murthy-lessons-from-flowers-the-japanese-concept-of-oubaitori/

~

**Pyt**

1. Anna Clarke, "Why the Danish art of 'pyt' could be the key to mastering mindfulness", *Vogue*, February 25, 2022, https://www.voguescandinavia.com/articles/pyt

2. Susan McQuillan, "Practice Pyt: A Natural Way to Reduce Stress", *Psychology Today*, May 1, 2023, https://www.psychologytoday.com/us/blog/cravings/202305/practice-pyt-a-natural-way-to-reduce-stress

3. Karen Rosinger, "What to do when hygge no longer works", *BBC*, 19 February 2019, https://www.bbc.com/travel/article/20190217-what-to-do-when-hygge-no-longer-works

4. Kristin Vuković, "The Danish tradition we all need now", *BBC*, 13 October 2022, https://www.bbc.com/travel/article/20221012-the-danish-tradition-we-all-need-now

5. Marie Helweg-Larsen, "A Danish word the world needs to combat stress: Pyt", *The Conversation*, February 27, 2019, https://scroll.in/article/914951/move-over-hygge-the-word-the-world-really-needs-to-combat-stress-is-danish-and-it-is-pyt

6. Kayleigh Dray, "Need a September reset? Try the Danish concept of 'pyt'", *Stylist,* 2024, https://www.stylist.co.uk/long-

reads/september-autumn-reset-danish-concept-pyt-psychology/
421160

7. Jessica Joelle Alexander, "Need to Hit the Reset Button? Try the Danish word "Pyt"", *The Danish Way of Parenting*, March 14, 2019, https://thedanishway.com/when-hygge-isnt-working-try-the-danish-word-pyt/

~

**Sisu**

1. *Wikipedia*, Sisu, https://en.wikipedia.org/wiki/Sisu

2. Anu Realo Ph.D., "Sisu: The Finnish Secret of Inner Strength and Resilience", *Psychology Today*, March 8, 2023, https://www.psychologytoday.com/intl/blog/the-quiet-joy-of-being/202303/sisu-the-finnish-secret-of-inner-strength-and-resilience

3. Olga Smirnova, "Sisu: The Finnish art of inner strength", *BBC*, 7 May 2018, https://www.bbc.com/worklife/article/20180502-sisu-the-finnish-art-of-inner-strength

4. Peter Marten, "The sisu within you: The Finnish key to life, love and success", *This is Finland*, March 2018, https://finland.fi/arts-culture/sisu-within-finnish-key-life-love-success/

5. Amy Beecham, "Sisu: how to embrace the Finnish art of inner strength and determination when the world feels in crisis", *Stylist*, 2022, https://www.stylist.co.uk/life/sisu-finnish-wellbeing-resilience-concept/686725

~

**Shinrin-yoku**

1. *Wikipedia*, Shinrin-yoku, https://en.wikipedia.org/wiki/Shinrin-yoku

2. Sunny Fitzgerald, "The secret to mindful travel? A walk in the woods", *National Geographic*, October 19, 2019, https://www.nationalgeographic.com/travel/article/forest-bathing-nature-walk-health

3. Harriet Sherwood, "Getting back to nature: how forest bathing can make us feel better", *The Guardian*, Sat 8 Jun 2019, https://www.theguardian.com/environment/2019/jun/08/forest-

bathing-japanese-practice-in-west-wellbeing

4. Susan Abookire, BSEE, MD, MPH, FACP, "Can forest therapy enhance health and well-being?", *Harvard Health Publishing (Harvard Medical School)*, May 29, 2020, https://www.health.harvard.edu/blog/can-forest-therapy-enhance-health-and-well-being-2020052919948

5. "What Is Forest Bathing and How Does it Benefit Mental and Physical Health?", *American Psychiatric Association*, December 22, 2023, https://www.psychiatry.org/news-room/apa-blogs/forest-bathing-benefits-mental-physical

6. Karin Evans, "Why Forest Bathing Is Good for Your Health", *Greater Good Magazine*, August 20, 2018, https://greatergood.berkeley.edu/article/item/why_forest_bathing_is_good_for_your_health

7. Team Cleveland Clinic, "Forest Bathing: What It Is and Its Potential Benefits", *Cleveland Clinic,* December 6, 2023, https://health.clevelandclinic.org/why-forest-therapy-can-be-good-for-your-body-and-mind

8. Team The Hike Collective, "Shinrin-Yoku: The Science Behind Forest Bathing", *The Hike Collective,* 16th July 2024, https://www.hikecollective.com.au/2024/07/16/shinrin-yoku-the-science-behind-forest-bathing/

9. Anthoni Oisin, BSc, "Forest Bathing for Health: How Nature Nurtures Wellbeing", *News Medical Life Sciences,* Last Updated: Oct 5, 2023, https://www.news-medical.net/health/Forest-Bathing-for-Health-How-Nature-Nurtures-Wellbeing.aspx

~

**Susegad**

1. *Wikipedia*, Susegad, https://en.wikipedia.org/wiki/Susegad

2. Charukesi Ramadurai, "India's 'all is well' approach to life", *BBC*, 8 July 2019, https://www.bbc.com/travel/article/20190708-indias-all-is-well-approach-to-life

3. Aparna Narrain, "Interpreting susegad", *The Hindu*, March 20, 2021, https://www.thehindu.com/life-and-style/travel/interpreting-susegad/article34110344.ece

# REFERENCES

~

**Ukeireru**

1. Scott Haas Ph.D., "How to Accept and Get Past Pain", *Psychology Today*, August 13, 2020, https://www.psychologytoday.com/intl/blog/shrink-in-the-kitchen/202008/how-to-accept-and-get-past-pain

2. Akiko Katayama, "Ukeireru: This Japanese Mindset May Be Key To Your Happiness", *Forbes*, Jul 12, 2020, https://www.forbes.com/sites/akikokatayama/2020/07/12/ukeireru-this-japanese-mindset-may-be-key-to-your-happiness/

3. George Blue Kelly, "Ukeireru–The Japanese Secret To Living Peacefully", *Medium*, Jun 20, 2021, https://medium.com/mind-cafe/ukeireru-the-japanese-secret-to-living-peacefully-47071ac6dd72

4. Sarah DiGiulio, "How to Adopt the Japanese Approach to Accepting Life's Challenges, "Ukeireru"", *Good Housekeeping*, Dec 08, 2020, https://www.goodhousekeeping.com/health/wellness/a34892924/ukeireru-how-to-accept-change/

5. Elizabeth Yuko, "How to Practice Ukeireru, the Japanese Art of Acceptance Through Awareness", *LifeHacker*, August 2, 2020, https://lifehacker.com/how-to-practice-ukeireru-the-japanese-art-of-acceptanc-1844581505

~

**Wabi-Sabi**

1. Wikipedia, Wabi-sabi, https://en.wikipedia.org/wiki/Wabi-sabi

2. Jo Nash, Ph.D. (Scientifically reviewed by Maike Neuhaus Ph.D.), "The Wabi Sabi Lifestyle: How to Accept Imperfection in Life", *Positive Psychology*, 15 Nov 2021, https://positivepsychology.com/wabi-sabi-lifestyle/

3. Omar Itani, "5 Teachings From The Japanese Wabi Sabi Philosophy That Can Drastically Improve Your Life", *Omar Itani Blog*, April 23, 2021, https://www.omaritani.com/blog/wabi-sabi-philosophy-teachings

4. Barbara Scoville, "Wabi Sabi: Find Peace by Embracing Flaws and Releasing Judgment", *Tiny Buddha,* https://tinybuddha.com/blog/wabi-sabi-find-peace-by-embracing-flaws-and-releasing-judgment/

5. Saniya Ahmad Khan, "Wabi-Sabi philosophy: Finding beauty in imperfection", *YourStory*, March 15, 2024, https://yourstory.com/2024/03/wabi-sabi-philosophy-daily-living

~


**Wu Wei**

1. *Wikipedia,* Wu wei, https://en.wikipedia.org/wiki/Wu_wei

2. Ying Hwa Kee, Chunxiao Li, Chun-Qing Zhang, John Chee Keng Wang, "The wu-wei alternative: Effortless action and non-striving in the context of mindfulness practice and performance in sport", *Asian Journal of Sport and Exercise Psychology, Volume 1, Issues 2–3, September–December 2021, Pages 122-132, https://www.sciencedirect.com/science/article/pii/S2667239121000319*

3. Edward Slingerland,"Wu-wei – doing less and wanting more", *The British Psychological Society*, 19 October 2015, https://www.bps.org.uk/psychologist/wu-wei-doing-less-and-wanting-more

4. Mark D. White Ph.D., "The Wisdom of Wei Wu Wei: Letting Good Things Happen", *Psychology Today*, July 9, 2011, https://www.psychologytoday.com/intl/blog/maybe-its-just-me/201107/the-wisdom-wei-wu-wei-letting-good-things-happen

5. Stephan Joppich, "The 2-Word Concept That Makes Everything You Do Feel Effortless", *Stephan Joppich Blog*, Jun 3, 2022, https://stephanjoppich.com/wu-wei/

6. Steve Christenson, "Origins of Happiness: Wu Wei", *My Best Self 101*, March 24, 2020, https://www.mybestself101.org/blog/2020/3/24/origins-of-happiness-wu-wei

7. Henrique Schneider, "Wu-Wei: Acting without Desire", *1000-Word Philosophy: An Introductory Anthology*, June 3, 2019, https://1000wordphilosophy.com/2019/06/03/wu-wei-acting-

without-desire/

# Author's Note

While reading a blog post about Niksen, I became intrigued by the idea of exploring similar concepts from across the world. This curiosity led me to delve into a journey in research on the theme of well-being through a linguistic perspective. My research deepened when I came across The Positive Lexicography Project which inspired and motivated me to keep working on the theme of finding calm and contentment in everyday moments as a vital part of maintaining overall well-being.

Life came full circle when I faced writer's block while finalizing the end matter for this book—partially because of the excitement of concluding the project I had been working on for the last three years, and partially due to the work stress that accompanied my constant research for it—a massive write-up that was now twenty-eight chapters strong and ready to take the shape of a book.

I am forever thankful to my fellow blogger, Sonia Dogra, whose blog post on Niksen sparked my curiosity, leading me to research and work on this book. Additionally, her valuable input was instrumental in completing the end matter of the book.

This book is a compilation of some blissful concepts that I learned while working in the field of well-being. The interpretations are my own, and I preferred to write emphasizing my experience of embracing and practicing these concepts, philosophies, and rituals rather than sharing detailed information about them.

It took me three years to learn, practice, and understand the benefits of following them. They significantly helped me in my well-being and thus, I conceived the idea of gathering these topics as a book that will help readers find calm and contentment in everyday moments.

If you are interested in learning more about them, please search for the resources in this book's 'References' section. You can search for more resources and learn them on your own. I wish you the best in your pursuit of calm and contentment!

# About The Author

A dreamer by heart and a seeker by soul, Swarnali Nath is an Engineer turned Digital Marketer turned full-time Writer. Her first book, **'Awaken the Story Within'**, received wide appreciation from readers and became a bestseller in Amazon's Spiritual Healing category. Her second book, **'A Letter to Tomorrow'** was much-loved and praised by its readers as the poetry and poetic pieces helped them in their healing journey.

She is the founder of **The Peace Stories** - an initiative to spread the message of hope, love, and peace to the world. A dedicated space for sharing positive and inspiring stories, this initiative also runs a campaign called 'There is still room for light' and collects and curates Notes on Peace. This initiative works on several projects: Letter to the Younger Self, The Strangers Connect, Of Peace and Purpose, Big Gratitude Jar, Reminders of Peace, You Matter, Journal Your Way, and more. Ellee, a baby elephant is the ambassador of this initiative. She sheds light on varied aspects of life and shares her messages on self-love.

Swarnali's blog, **The Blissful Storyteller**, has been featured among the top 100 blogs on the web in the categories of Mindfulness and Storytelling. It is one of the top blogs from India and across the globe. The blog is a potpourri of her researched articles on small acts of transformation that help in taking care of your mental and emotional well-being and finding calm in everyday moments. Her articles have been featured on the leading online platforms in India.

A two-time awardee of the prestigious Orange Flower Awards in the category of Wellness and fitness, Swarnali is passionate about her work as a Well-being Researcher and Storyteller. A coffee lover, a prolific writer, and an avid reader, she finds solace in books and music. Get in touch with her on Instagram @blissfulstoryteller and Twitter @scarsandglory.

# Also By The Author

Awaken the Story Within: A Journey to Rekindle the Lamp of Heart (Kindle Edition Published in 2020, Paperback Edition Published in 2023. Publisher: Notion Press)
A Letter to Tomorrow: My Learnings from the Days of Despair to Welcome the Daybreak of Peace and Purpose (Kindle Edition Published in 2021, Paperback Edition Published in 2023. Publisher: Notion Press)

# Praise For The Book

"I loved reading about the series titled 'Art of Life', especially for the theme chosen to curate these wonderful concepts. It's meaningful and necessary for all of us. The concepts presented in the book are relatable and simple to follow if we are looking to de-stress our lives. I appreciate the way the author has blended the concepts with her poetic narrative!

*- Radhika Acharya, Author, TOI Blogger*

"Each chapter of this book has been adding to my curiosity as to what new concept, what new word will the author bring to the platter next! I must say, she has served us with a delectable spread. With the newly learned concepts, I have added a lot of positive thoughts and beautiful words to my dictionary. These positive thoughts are beneficial in embracing peace and happiness in daily life. I am thinking of making a calendar of these concepts and following the day with the positivity of the word of the day! Once again, I thank the author for bringing this beautiful series. I wish her all the best for her book."

*- Anagha Yatin, Writer, Nomad, Arts and Crafts Enthusiast*

"We often wait for something big to happen in our lives, forgetting that it is the little things that make life worth living. Thanks to the author for bringing this gentle reminder to us through her book."

*- Sonia Dogra, Writer & Freelance Editor*

"In the anticipation of something big, we forget to enjoy the small things in life. Reading this book, I realized I should carry a book or my laptop to the garden below, to read or to pen my thoughts amongst the plants on the swings, and watch young kids and puppies play around me. That could be an enjoyable experience. Thanks to the author for this beautiful book which

taught me to celebrate little things in my life."
    *- Aesha Shah, Career Counsellor and Blogger*

"The author's words seemed like a ray of sunshine. In this book, she has written that happiness is a journey and I believe it wholeheartedly. I wish her all the very best in the pursuit of happiness!"
    *- Harshita Nanda, Writer*

"To feel every pulse of happiness is a true boon! May we all feel this way. Thanks to the author for teaching us some beautiful words with their equally beautiful meanings."
    *- Deepti Menon, Author and Educator*

"Enjoying life is an art. This wonderful book presents the basic ingredients of that art."
    *- Tomichan Matheikal, Teacher, Blogger, Author and Passionate Seeker of Wisdom*